Pint Size Traditions II

by Lynette Jensen

Just like puppies and kitties, small quilts

steal your heart. The following pages

will guide you effortlessly to create

many charming Pint Size Quilts.

CONTENTS

Simple changes in accessorizing can make a dramatic difference by using colored pottery and collectibles with your Pint Size Quilts.

Radiant Star

Radiant Star

24-inches square

Before beginning this project, read through Getting Started on page 95.

Fabrics and Supplies

1/4 yard **RED DIAGONAL PRINT** for star section

1/2 yard **BEIGE PRINT** for background and pieced border

3/8 yard **RED PRINT** for nine-patch blocks, inner border, and pieced border

1/4 yard **GREEN PRINT** for triangle-pieced squares, corner squares, and pieced border

3/8 yard **GOLD/GREEN DIAGONAL PRINT** for outer border

1/3 yard **RED DIAGONAL PRINT** for binding

7/8 yard for backing

quilt batting, at least 30-inches square

nine-patch blocks

Makes 4 blocks

Cutting

From **BEIGE PRINT**:
- Cut 1, 1-7/8 x 42-inch strip
- Cut 2 to 3, 1-1/2 x 42-inch strips. From the strips cut:
  - 1, 1-1/2 x 15-inch strip
  - 2, 1-1/2 x 8-inch strips
  - 16, 1-1/2 x 3-1/2-inch rectangles

From **RED PRINT**:
- Cut 1, 1-1/2 x 42-inch strip. From the strip cut:
  - 2, 1-1/2 x 15-inch strips
  - 1, 1-1/2 x 8-inch strip

From **GREEN PRINT**:
- Cut 1, 1-7/8 x 42-inch strip

Piecing

Step 1 Aligning long edges, sew a 1-1/2 x 15-inch **RED** strip to both side edges of the 1-1/2 x 15-inch **BEIGE** strip; press. Cut the strip set into segments.

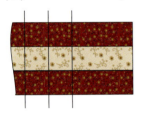

Crosscut 8, 1-1/2-inch wide segments

Step 2 Aligning long edges, sew a 1-1/2 x 8-inch **BEIGE** strip to both side edges of the 1-1/2 x 8-inch **RED** strip; press. Cut the strip set into segments.

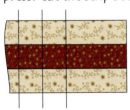

Crosscut 4, 1-1/2-inch wide segments

Step 3 Sew Step 1 segments to both edges of a Step 2 segment; press. Sew 1-1/2 x 3-1/2-inch **BEIGE** rectangles to the top/bottom edges of each nine-patch block. At this point each nine-patch unit should measure 3-1/2 x 5-1/2-inches.

Make 4

Make 4

Step 4 Layer together the 1-7/8 x 42-inch **GREEN** and **BEIGE** strips. Press together, but do not sew. Cut the layered strip into squares. Cut each layered square in half diagonally to make 16 sets of triangles. Stitch 1/4-inch from the diagonal edge of each pair of triangles; press.

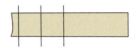

Crosscut 8, 1-7/8-inch squares

Make 16, 1-1/2-inch triangle-pieced squares

Step 5 Sew triangle-pieced squares to both ends of a 1-1/2 x 3-1/2-inch **BEIGE** rectangle; press. Make 8 units. Sew the units to the side edges of the nine-patch units; press. At this point each nine-patch block should measure 5-1/2-inches square.

Make 4

star section and quilt center

Cutting

From **RED DIAGONAL PRINT**:
- Cut 1, 2-1/2 x 42-inch strip. From the strip cut:
  - 1, 2-1/2 x 4-1/2-inch rectangle
  - 2, 1-1/2 x 2-1/2-inch rectangles
- Cut 1, 1-1/2 x 42-inch strip. From the strip cut:
  - 8, 1-1/2 x 3-1/2-inch rectangles
  - 8, 1-1/2-inch squares

From **BEIGE PRINT**:
- Cut 1, 1-1/2 x 42-inch strip. From the strip cut:
  - 4, 1-1/2 x 2-1/2-inch rectangles
  - 16, 1-1/2-inch squares

*Note: Refer to page 99 for **Chain Piecing** instructions.*

Piecing

Step 1 Position a 1-1/2-inch **BEIGE** square on the corner of a 1-1/2 x 3-1/2-inch **RED DIAGONAL PRINT** rectangle. Draw a diagonal line on the square and stitch on the line. Trim the seam allowances to 1/4-inch; press. Repeat this process at the opposite corner of the rectangle. Make 4 units. Reverse the direction of the stitching lines to make 4 more units. Sew the units together in pairs to make star point units; press.

Make 4

Make 4

Make 4

Step 2 Position a 1-1/2-inch **RED DIAGONAL PRINT** square on the corner of a 1-1/2 x 2-1/2-inch **BEIGE** rectangle. Draw a diagonal line on the square; stitch, trim, and press. Repeat this process at the opposite corner of the rectangle. Make 4 units. Sew 2 of the units to the ends of the 2-1/2 x 4-1/2-inch **RED DIAGONAL PRINT** rectangle; press. Then add a Step 1 star point unit to both ends of the unit; press. At this point the star center section should measure 2-1/2 x 12-1/2-inches.

Make 4

Make 1

Step 3 Sew the remaining Step 2 units to the 1-1/2 x 2-1/2-inch **RED DIAGONAL PRINT** rectangles; press. Sew the remaining Step 1 star point units to these units; press. At this point each unit should measure 2-1/2 x 5-1/2-inches.

Make 2

Step 4 Sew the nine-patch blocks to both edges of the Step 3 units; press. At this point each section should measure 5-1/2 x 12-1/2-inches.

Make 2

Step 5 Referring to the quilt diagram on page 5 for placement, sew the Step 4 sections to both side edges of the Step 2 star center section; press. At this point the quilt center should measure 12-1/2-inches square.

borders

*Note: The yardage given allows for the border strips to be cut on the crosswise grain. Read through **Border** instructions on page 100 for general instructions on adding borders.*

Cutting

From **RED PRINT**:
- Cut 1, 2-1/2 x 42-inch strip. From the strip cut:
     4, 2-1/2-inch corner squares
- Cut 2, 1-1/2 x 42-inch inner border strips
- Cut 2 more 1-1/2 x 42-inch strips. From the strips cut:
     24, 1-1/2 x 2-1/2-inch rectangles

From **GREEN PRINT**:
- Cut 2 to 3, 1-1/2 x 42-inch strips. From the strips cut:
     32, 1-1/2 x 2-1/2-inch rectangles
     4, 1-1/2-inch corner squares

From **BEIGE PRINT**:
- Cut 4, 1-1/2 x 42-inch strips. From the strips cut: 112, 1-1/2-inch squares

From **GOLD/GREEN DIAGONAL PRINT**:
- Cut 3, 3-1/2 x 42-inch outer border strips

Assembling and Attaching the Borders

Step 1 Attach the 1-1/2-inch wide **RED** top/bottom inner border strips; press. For the side borders, measure just the quilt top including seam allowances, but not the top/bottom borders. Cut the 1-1/2-inch wide **RED** side inner border strips to this length. Sew a 1-1/2-inch **GREEN** corner square to both ends of the border strips; press. Sew the border strips to the side edges of the quilt center; press.

Step 2 Position a 1-1/2-inch **BEIGE** square on the corner of a 1-1/2 x 2-1/2-inch **GREEN** rectangle. Draw a diagonal line on the **BEIGE** square; stitch, trim, and press. Repeat this process at the opposite corner of the rectangle. Make 16 units. Reverse the direction of the stitching lines to make 16 more units. Sew the units together in pairs to make the **GREEN** units; press.

Make 16

Make 16   Make 16

Step 3 Position a 1-1/2-inch **BEIGE** square on the corner of a 1-1/2 x 2-1/2-inch **RED** rectangle. Draw a diagonal line on the **BEIGE** square; stitch, trim, and press. Repeat this process at the opposite corner of the rectangle. Make 12 units. Reverse the direction of the stitching lines to make 12 more units. Sew the units together in pairs to make the **RED** units; press.

Make 12

Make 12   Make 12

Step 4 For each pieced border, sew together 4 of the **GREEN** units and 3 of the **RED** units; press. At this point each pieced border should measure 2-1/2 x 14-1/2-inches.

Make 4

Step 5 Sew pieced borders to the top/bottom edges of the quilt center; press. Sew 2-1/2-inch **RED** corner squares to the remaining pieced borders; press. Sew the pieced borders to the side edges of the quilt center; press.

Step 6 Attach the 3-1/2-inch wide **GOLD/GREEN DIAGONAL PRINT** outer border strips.

putting it all together

Trim the backing and batting so they are 6-inches larger than the quilt top. Refer to **Finishing the Quilt** on page 100 for complete instructions.

QUILTING SUGGESTIONS:
- Log Cabin blocks - crosshatch
- **RED** and **GREEN** corner squares - big X and in-the-ditch
- Star-echo in **RED** and **BEIGE** areas and in-the-ditch around star
- Chevron border - **RED/GREEN** - echo and in-the-ditch
- **BEIGE** stipple
- **RED** inner border - in-the-ditch
- Outer border - 1" channel stitching

binding

Cutting

From **RED DIAGONAL PRINT**:
- Cut 3, 2-3/4 x 42-inch strips

Sew the binding to the quilt using a 3/8-inch seam allowance. This measurement will produce a 1/2-inch wide finished double binding. Refer to **Binding** and **Diagonal Piecing** on page 101 for complete instructions.

Folk Art houses, antique or newly
made are great accessories
for Pint Size quilts.

Winterfest

Winterfest

27-inches square

Before beginning this project, read through Getting Started on page 95.

Fabrics and Supplies

1/4 yard **GOLD PRINT** for log cabin center squares and stars

1/3 yard **GREEN PRINT** for log cabin blocks and quilt center

3/8 yard **DARK RED PRINT** for log cabin blocks, quilt center, and middle border

1/4 yard **BLACK PRINT #1** for applique foundation squares and snowman eye appliques

5/8 yard **BLACK PRINT #2** for quilt center, inner and outer border

1/8 yard **GOLD w/RED FLORAL** for quilt center and snowman scarf appliques

1/8 yard **CREAM PRINT** for snowman and snowflake appliques

4-inch square **LIGHT RED PRINT** for snowman nose appliques

1/3 yard **GOLD w/RED FLORAL** for binding

1 yard for backing

quilt batting, at least 33-inches square

pearl cotton or machine-embroidery thread for decorative stitches: black, gold

paper-backed fusible web

tear-away fabric stabilizer for applique

optional black buttons for eyes (1/2-inch)

log cabin blocks

Makes 4 blocks

Cutting

From **GOLD PRINT**:
- Cut 1, 1-1/2 x 10-inch strip

From **GREEN PRINT**:
- Cut 3, 1 x 42-inch strips
  From one of the the strips cut:
  2, 1 x 10-inch strips

From **DARK RED PRINT**:
- Cut 3, 1 x 42-inch strips

Piecing

Step 1 1 Aligning long edges, sew a 1 x 10-inch **GREEN** strip to both side edges of the 1-1/2 x 10-inch **GOLD** strip; press. Cut the strip set into segments.

Crosscut 4, 1-1/2-inch wide segments

Step 2 Sew 1-inch wide **DARK RED** strips to the side edges of the unit; press. Trim the strips even with the edges of the unit.

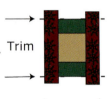

Trim

Step 3 Sew 1-inch wide **GREEN** strips to the top/bottom edges of the unit; press and trim.

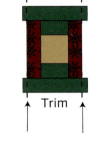

Trim

Step 4 Referring to the block diagram, continue adding the 1-inch wide **DARK RED** and **GREEN** strips to complete the log cabin block. Press and trim each strip before adding the next. Each log cabin block should measure 4 -1/2-inches square when complete. Adjust the seam allowances if needed.

Make 4

FUSIBLE WEB APPLIQUE METHOD

Cutting

From **BLACK PRINT #1**:
- Cut 1, 4-1/2 x 42-inch strip. From the strip cut:
  5, 4-1/2-inch applique foundation squares

Prepare the Appliques

Step 1 Make templates using the shapes on page 15. Trace the shapes on the paper side of the fusible web, leaving a small margin between each one. Cut the shapes apart.

Note: When you are fusing a large shape, like the snowman, fuse just the outer edges of the shape so that it will not look stiff when finished. To do this, draw a line about 3/8-inch inside the snowman, and cut away the fusible web on this line.

Step 2 Following the manufacturer's instructions, fuse the shapes to the wrong side of the fabric chosen for the appliques. Let the fabric cool and cut along the traced line. Peel away the paper backing from the fusible web.

Step 3 Referring to the block diagrams, position the shapes on the 4-1/2-inch **BLACK #1** applique foundation squares; fuse in place.

Step 4 We machine blanket stitched around the snowflake and snowman shapes using black machine embroidery thread. Gold thread was used to blanket stitch around the scarves. If you like, you could hand blanket stitch around the shapes with pearl cotton. The snowman's mouth was straight stitched with black thread.

Note: When machine stitching the appliques in place, we suggest pinning a rectangle of tear-away stabilizer to the backside of the block so it will lay flat when the applique is complete. We use the extra-lightweight Easy Tear™ sheets as a stabilizer. When the applique is complete, tear away the stabilizer.

Blanket Stitch

Straight Stitch

quilt center

Cutting

From **GOLD PRINT**:
- Cut 1, 1-1/2 x 42-inch strip. From the strip cut:
  16, 1-1/2-inch squares
- Cut 4, 1 x 42-inch strips. From the strips cut:
  128, 1-inch squares

From **DARK RED PRINT**:
- Cut 1, 2-1/2 x 42-inch strip. From the strip cut:
  6, 2-1/2 x 4-1/2-inch rectangles
- Cut 2, 1-1/2 x 42-inch strips. From the strips cut:
  12, 1-1/2 x 4-1/2-inch rectangles

From **GREEN PRINT**:
- Cut 1, 2-1/2 x 42-inch strip. From the strip cut:
  6, 2-1/2 x 4-1/2-inch rectangles
- Cut 2, 1-1/2 x 42-inch strips. From the strips cut:
  12, 1-1/2 x 4-1/2-inch rectangles

From **BLACK PRINT #2**:
- Cut 1, 1-1/2 x 42-inch strip. From the strip cut:
  16, 1-1/2 x 2-1/2-inch rectangles

From **GOLD w/RED FLORAL**:
- Cut 1, 2-1/2 x 14-inch strip. From the strip cut:
  4, 2-1/2-inch squares

Piecing and Quilt Center Assembly

Step 1 With right sides together, position a 1-inch **GOLD** square on the corner of a 1-1/2 x 4-1/2-inch **DARK RED** rectangle. Draw a diagonal line on the square and stitch on the line. Trim the seam allowance to 1/4-inch; press. Repeat this process at the adjacent corner of the rectangle. Repeat this process at the opposite end of the rectangle

Make 12 pieced
lattice units

Step 2 Referring to Step 1, sew 1-inch **GOLD** squares to the 4 corners of the 1-1/2 x 4-1/2-inch **GREEN** rectangles; press.

Make 12 pieced
lattice units

Step 3 With right sides together, position a 1-inch **GOLD** square on the corner of a 1-1/2 x 2-1/2-inch **BLACK #2** rectangle. Draw a diagonal line on the square, stitch, trim, and press. Repeat this process at the adjacent corner of the rectangle.

Make 16 pieced
lattice units

Step 4 Sew 4 of the **DARK RED** pieced lattice units, 2 of the snowman blocks, and 1 of the log cabin blocks together; press. At this point each block row should measure 4-1/2 x 16-1/2-inches.

Make 2 block rows

Step 5 Sew together 4 of the **DARK RED** pieced lattice units, the snowflake block, and 2 of the log cabin blocks; press. At this point the block row should measure 4-1/2 x 16-1/2-inches.

Make 1 block row

Step 6 Sew together 4 of the 1-1/2-inch **GOLD** squares and 3 of the **GREEN** pieced lattice units; press. At this point each lattice strip should measure 1-1/2 x 16-1/2-inches.

Make 4 lattice strips

Step 7 Referring to the quilt center assembly diagram on page 14, sew the block rows and lattice strips together; press. At this point the quilt center should measure 16-1/2-inches square.

Deck The Halls

Deck The Halls

14-inches square

Before beginning this project, read through Getting Started on page 95.

Fabrics and Supplies

1/8 yard **GREEN/RED FLORAL** for tree block

1/8 yard **BEIGE PRINT** for tree blocks

3 x 6-inch piece **BLACK PRINT** for tree stand

1/8 yard **RED PRINT** for inner border

1/4 yard **GOLD PRINT** for outer border and star applique

1/3 yard **GREEN LEAF PRINT** for prairie points and corner squares

1/4 yard **RED PRINT** for binding

5/8 yard for backing

quilt batting, at least 20-inches square

paper-backed fusible web

tear-away fabric stabilizer

machine embroidery thread or pearl cotton for decorative stitches: black

1/4-inch diameter bells (16)

tree block

Cutting

From GREEN/RED FLORAL:
- Cut 1, 2-1/2 x 20-inch strip.
  From the strip cut:
  1, 2-1/2 x 6-1/2-inch rectangle
  2, 2-1/2-inch squares
- Cut 1, 1-1/2 x 20-inch strip.
  From the strip cut:
  1, 1-1/2 x 6-1/2-inch rectangle
  1, 1-1/2 x 4-1/2-inch rectangle

From BEIGE PRINT:
- Cut 1, 3-1/2 x 42-inch strip.
  From the strip cut:
  2, 3-1/2 x 4-1/2-inch rectangles
  2, 2-1/2 x 3-1/2-inch rectangles
  4, 1-1/2 x 3-1/2-inch rectangles
  2, 1-1/2 x 2-1/2-inch rectangles

From BLACK PRINT:
- Cut 1, 1-1/2 x 4-1/2-inch rectangle

Piecing

Step 1 With right sides together, position a 2-1/2-inch **GREEN/RED FLORAL** square on the lower right corner of a 3-1/2 x 4-1/2-inch **BEIGE** rectangle. Draw a diagonal line on the square and stitch on the line. Trim the seam allowance to 1/4-inch; press.

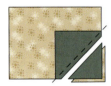 

Make 1

Step 2 With right sides together, position a 2-1/2-inch **GREEN/RED FLORAL** square on the lower left corner of a 3-1/2 x 4-1/2-inch **BEIGE** rectangle. Draw a diagonal line on the square; stitch, trim, and press.

Make 1

Step 3 Sew together the Step 1 and Step 2 units; press. At this point the tree top unit should measure 3-1/2 x 8-1/2-inches.

Make 1

Step 4 With right sides together, position 1-1/2 x 3-1/2-inch **BEIGE** rectangles on both corners of the 1-1/2 x 4-1/2-inch **GREEN/RED FLORAL** rectangle. Draw a diagonal line on the **BEIGE** rectangles; stitch, trim, and press. At this point the unit should measure 1-1/2 x 8-1/2-inches.

Make 1

Step 5 With right sides together, position 2-1/2 x 3-1/2-inch **BEIGE** rectangles on both corners of the 2-1/2 x 6-1/2-inch **GREEN/RED FLORAL** rectangle. Draw a diagonal line on the **BEIGE** rectangles; stitch, trim, and press. At this point the unit should measure 2-1/2 x 8-1/2-inches.

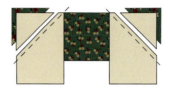 

Make 1

Step 6 With right sides together, position 1-1/2 x 2-1/2-inch **BEIGE** rectangles on both corners of the 1-1/2 x 6-1/2-inch **GREEN/RED FLORAL** rectangle. Draw a diagonal line on the **BEIGE** rectangles; stitch, trim, and press. At this point the unit should measure 1-1/2 x 8-1/2-inches.

Make 1

Step 7 With right sides together, position 1-1/2 x 3-1/2-inch **BEIGE** rectangles on both corners of the 1-1/2 x 4-1/2-inch **BLACK** rectangle. Draw a diagonal line on the **BEIGE** rectangles; stitch, trim, and press. At this point the tree stand unit should measure 1-1/2 x 8-1/2-inches.

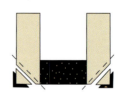 

Make 1

Step 8 Referring to the tree block diagram for placement, sew together the Step 3 through 7 units; press. At this point the tree block should measure 8-1/2-inches square.

Step 3

Step 4

Step 5

Step 6

Step 7

borders

Note: *The yardage given allows for the border strips to be cut on the crosswise grain. Refer to* **Border** *instructions on page 100 for general instructions on adding borders.*

Cutting

From **RED PRINT**:
- Cut 1, 1-1/2 x 42-inch inner border strip

From **GOLD PRINT**:
- Cut 1, 2-1/2 x 42-inch outer border strip

From **GREEN LEAF PRINT**:
- Cut 2, 4 x 42-inch strips. From the strips cut:
      16, 4-inch squares (set aside to
            be used for prairie point trim)
      4, 2-1/2-inch corner squares

Attaching the Borders

Step 1 Attach the 1-1/2-inch wide **RED** inner border strips.

Step 2 Attach the 2-1/2-inch wide top/bottom **GOLD** outer border strips.

Step 3 For the side borders, measure the quilt from top to bottom, including the seam allowances but not the borders just added. Cut the 2-1/2-inch wide **GOLD** side outer border strips to this length. Sew 2-1/2-inch **GREEN LEAF PRINT** corner squares to both ends of the border strips; press. Sew the border strips to the side edges of the quilt center.

APPLIQUE FUSIBLE WEB METHOD

Step 1 Make template using the shape below. Trace the shape on the paper side of the fusible web.

Step 2 Following the manufacturer's instructions, fuse the shape to the wrong side of the fabric chosen for the applique. Let the fabric cool and cut along the traced line. Peel away the paper backing from the fusible web. Position the star applique shape on the quilt top.

Note: *We suggest pinning a square of tear-away stabilizer to the backside of the quilt top so it will lay flat when the machine applique is complete.*

Step 3 We machine blanket stitched around the shape using black machine embroidery thread. If you like, you could hand blanket stitch around the shape with pearl cotton.

Blanket Stitch

Note: *To prevent the hand blanket stitches from "rolling off" the edges of the applique shape, take an extra backstitch in the same place as you made the blanket stitch, going around the outer curves, corners, and points. For straight edges, taking a backstitch every inch is enough.*

Star
Trace 1
onto fusible
web

putting it all together

Trim the backing and batting so they are 6-inches larger than the quilt top. The project will need to be quilted before the Prairie Point Trim is added. Refer to **Finishing the Quilt** on page 100 for complete instructions.

QUILTING SUGGESTIONS:

- Tree - echo quilt boughs.
- **BEIGE** background - crosshatch.
- In-the-ditch quilting - around tree, star, base, and **RED** inner border
- **GOLD** outer border - channel stitching.
- **GREEN** corner squares - big X.

prairie point trim

Step 1 Fold a 4-inch **GREEN LEAF PRINT** square (cut previously) in half diagonally, wrong sides together; press. Fold the triangle in half again; press.

Step 2 Referring to the quilt diagram on page 17, pin 4 prairie points to each **GOLD** border, overlapping then slightly. Adjust the prairie points to fit the border and baste them in place with a scant 1/4-inch seam allowance. Repeat this procedure for all 4 sides of the quilt.

Step 3 Make a few stitches at the point of each prairie point to secure it to the quilt top. Sew a decorative bell in place.

binding

Cutting

From **RED PRINT**:
- Cut 2, 3 x 42-inch strips

Note: The binding for this project is cut a bit wider since it will be going around extra layers of fabric.

Sew the binding to the quilt (encasing the raw edges of the prairie points) using a 3/8-inch seam allowance. This measurement will produce a 1/2-inch wide finished double binding. Refer to **Binding** and **Diagonal Piecing** on page 101 for complete instructions.

Carry the holiday theme throughout your home. No need to be extravagant - place greens and berries in a garden urn for a festive holiday arrangement.

A collection of santas on a tiered wooden spool shelf will bring a nostalgic touch to a corner of your home. A grouping of small like items makes a large decorative statement.

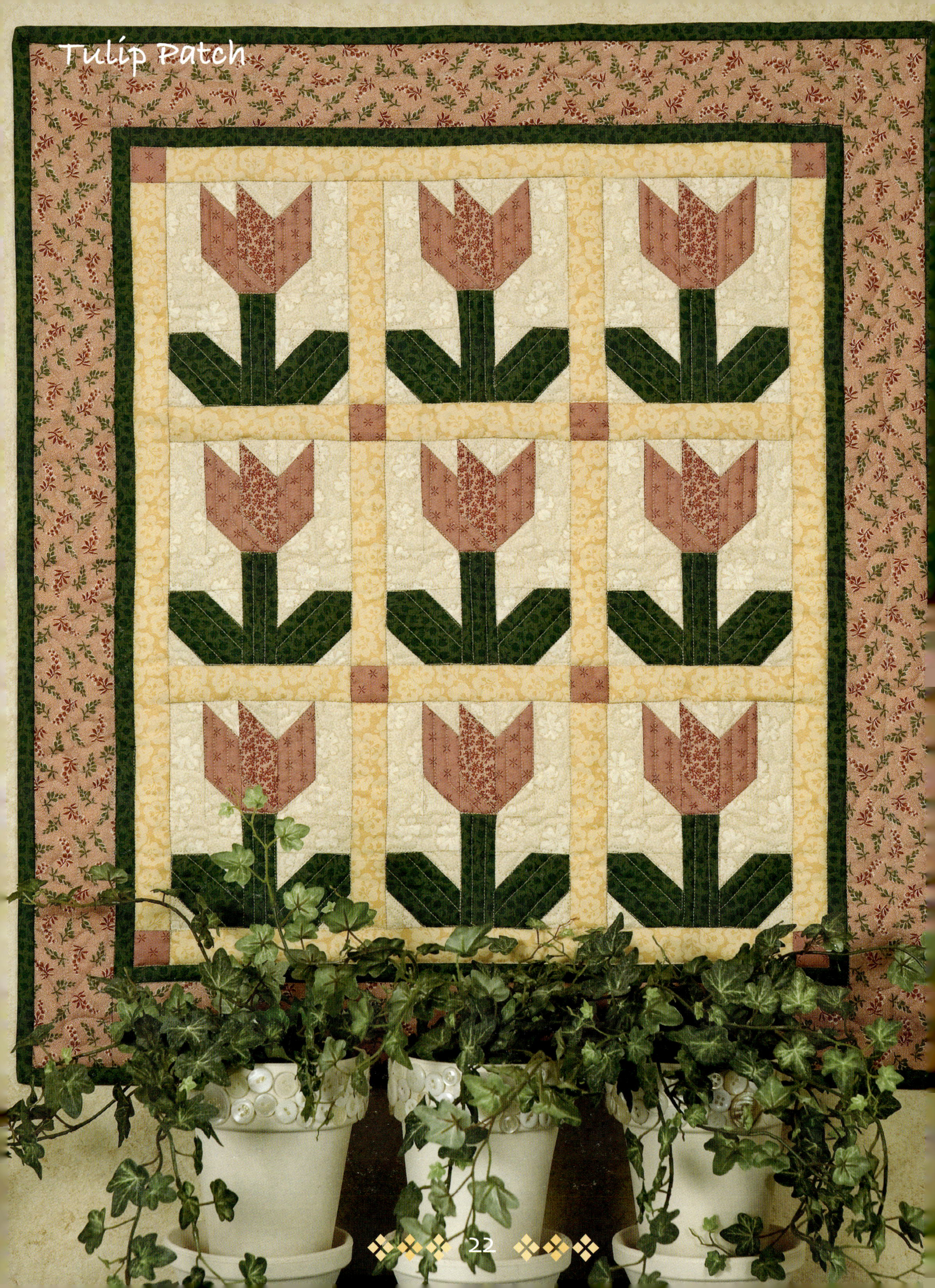
Tulip Patch

Tulip Patch

25 x 28-inches

Before beginning this project, read through Getting Started on page 95.

Fabrics and Supplies

1/4 yard **ROSE PRINT #1** for outer tulip petals and lattice posts/corner squares

1/8 yard **ROSE PRINT #2** for inner tulip petals

1/3 yard **BEIGE PRINT** for block background

3/8 yard **GREEN PRINT** for blocks and middle border

1/4 yard **YELLOW PRINT** for lattice strips and inner border

1/3 yard **ROSE/GREEN FLORAL** for outer border

1/3 yard **GREEN PRINT** for binding

7/8 yard for backing

quilt batting, at least 31 x 34-inches

Pumpkin House

23 x 27-inches

Before beginning this project, read through Getting Started on page 95.

Fabrics and Supplies

1/4 yard **CHESTNUT PRINT** for house and inner border

4 x 14-inch piece **DARK GOLD PRINT** for windows

1/2 yard **BLACK PRINT** for house, quilt center, pumpkin units, and picket fence border

1/8 yard **LIGHT GOLD PRINT** for star points

1/2 yard **GREEN PRINT** for house, pumpkin stems, and outer border

1/8 yard **ORANGE/BLACK PRINT** for star center and outer pumpkin units

3 x 20-inch piece **DARK ORANGE PRINT** for star center and inner pumpkin units

1/4 yard **TAN PRINT** for picket fence border

1/4 yard **CHESTNUT PRINT** for binding

7/8 yard for backing

quilt batting, at least 29 x 33-inches

quilt center

Cutting

From **CHESTNUT PRINT**:
- Cut 1, 2 x 42-inch strip. From the strip cut:
  - 2, 2-inch squares
  - 2, 1-1/2 x 4-3/8-inch rectangles
  - 2, 1-1/2 x 2-inch rectangles
  - 2, 1-1/4 x 5-1/2-inch rectangles
- Cut 1, 1 x 42-inch strip. From the strip cut:
  - 2, 1 x 5-1/2-inch rectangles
  - 6, 1 x 2-inch rectangles
  - 12, 1-inch squares

From **DARK GOLD PRINT**:
- Cut 1, 2 x 14-inch strip. From the strip cut:
  - 5, 2-inch squares
  - 1, 1 x 1-1/2-inch rectangle

From **BLACK PRINT**:
- Cut 1, 3 x 42-inch strip. From the strip cut:
  - 2, 3 x 13-1/2-inch rectangles
- Cut 1, 2 x 42-inch strip. From the strip cut:
  - 3, 2 x 3-1/2-inch rectangles
  - 2, 2 x 3-inch rectangles
  - 2, 2-inch squares
- Cut 1, 1-1/2 x 42-inch strip. From the strip cut:
  - 2, 1-1/2 x 4-3/8-inch rectangles
  - 2, 1 x 12-1/2-inch border strips
- Cut 1, 1 x 42-inch strip. From the strip cut:
  - 2, 1 x 5-inch rectangles
  - 2, 1 x 3-inch rectangles
  - 1, 1 x 1-1/2-inch rectangle
  - 21, 1-inch squares

From **LIGHT GOLD PRINT**:
- Cut 1, 2-3/8 x 42-inch strip. From the strip cut:
  - 2, 2-3/8 x 4-3/8-inch rectangles
  - 6, 2-inch squares

From **GREEN PRINT**:
- Cut 1, 4-3/8 x 42-inch strip. From the strip cut:
  - 2, 4-3/8-inch squares
  - 1, 2 x 7-1/2-inch rectangle
  - 2, 2-inch squares
  - 8, 1-inch squares

From **ORANGE/BLACK PRINT**:
- Cut 2, 1-1/2 x 42-inch strips. From the strips cut:
  - 10, 1-1/2 x 3-1/2-inch rectangles
  - 12, 1-inch squares

From **DARK ORANGE PRINT**:
- Cut 1, 1-1/2 x 20-inch strip. From the strip cut:
  - 5, 1-1/2 x 3-1/2-inch rectangles

Quilt Center Assembly

Step 1 To make the window units, with right sides together, position 1-inch **CHESTNUT** squares on the upper corners of a 2-inch **DARK GOLD** square. Draw a diagonal line on the small squares; stitch on the lines. Trim the seam allowances to 1/4-inch; press.

Make 5 window units

Step 2 To make the door unit, sew together a 1-inch **BLACK** square, a 1 x 1-1/2-inch **DARK GOLD** rectangle, and a 1 x 1-1/2-inch **BLACK** rectangle; press. Sew 1 x 3-inch **BLACK** rectangles to the side edges of the unit; press. With right sides together, position 2 of the 1-inch **CHESTNUT** squares on the upper corners of the unit. Draw a diagonal line on the squares; stitch, trim, and press. At this point the door unit should measure 2 x 3-inches.

Make 1 door unit

Step 3 Sew together 2 of the window units, 2 of the 1 x 2-inch **CHESTNUT** rectangles, and 1 of the 1-1/2 x 2-inch **CHESTNUT** rectangles; press. At this point each window unit should measure 2 x 5-1/2-inches.

Make 2 window units

Step 4 Sew together 1 of the window units, 2 of the 1 x 2-inch **CHESTNUT** rectangles, and the door unit; press. At this point the door/window unit should measure 2 x 5-1/2-inches.

Make 1 door/window unit

Step 5 Referring to the diagram, sew together the window units, the door/window unit, and the 1 x 5-1/2-inch **CHESTNUT** rectangles; press. Sew the 1-1/4 x 5-1/2-inch **CHESTNUT** rectangles to the side edges of the unit; press. At this point the house base should measure 5-1/2 x 7-1/2-inches.

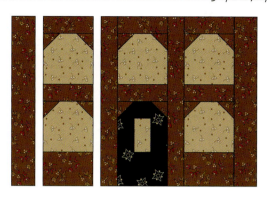

Step 6 To prepare the roof unit, aligning long edges, sew together a 1-1/2 x 4-3/8-inch **CHESTNUT** rectangle, a 1-1/2 x 4-3/8-inch **BLACK** rectangle, and a 2-3/8 x 4-3/8-inch **LIGHT GOLD** rectangle; press. Make 2 units. At this point each unit should measure 4-3/8-inches square.

Make 2

Step 7 To make the left roof top unit refer to the diagrams. Position a 4-3/8-inch **GREEN** square on a Step 6 unit (be sure the **LIGHT GOLD** strip is on the right hand side). Cut the layered squares diagonally in half (notice the direction of the cutting line). Stitch 1/4-inch from the diagonal edge; press. Position a 2-inch **CHESTNUT** square on the lower right corner of the pieced square. Draw a diagonal line on the small square; stitch, trim, and press. At this point the left roof top unit should measure 4-inches square.

 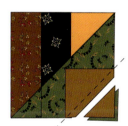 

Make 1 left roof top unit

Step 8 To make the right roof top unit refer to the diagrams. Position a 4-3/8-inch **GREEN** square on a Step 6 unit (be sure the **LIGHT GOLD** strip is on the left hand side). Cut the layered squares diagonally in half (notice the direction of the cutting line). Stitch 1/4-inch from the diagonal edge; press. Position a 2-inch **CHESTNUT** square on the lower left corner of the pieced square. Draw a diagonal line on the small square; stitch, trim, and press. At this point the right roof top unit should measure 4-inches square.

 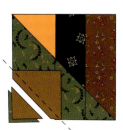 

Make 1 right roof top unit

Step 9 Sew together the 2 roof top units; press. Referring to the quilt center diagram on page 33, sew the roof unit to the house base unit; press. At this point the quilt center should measure 7-1/2 x 9-inches.

Make 1 roof top unit

Step 10 To make the star center unit, with right sides together, position 1-inch **ORANGE/BLACK PRINT** squares on 2 opposite corners of a 1-1/2 x 3-1/2-inch **DARK ORANGE** rectangle. Draw a diagonal line on the squares; stitch, trim, and press. Repeat this process at the remaining corners of the rectangle. Make 1 unit. Sew 1-1/2 x 3-1/2-inch **ORANGE/BLACK PRINT** rectangles to both side edges of the unit; press. With right sides together, position 1-inch **BLACK** squares on the corners of the unit. Draw diagonal lines on the squares; stitch, trim, and press. At this point the star center unit should measure 3-1/2-inches square.

Make 1

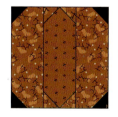

Make 1 star center

Step 11 The pumpkin corner blocks are made in the same manner as the Step 10 star center. Position a 1-inch **GREEN** square on the upper left corner of a 1-1/2 x 3-1/2-inch **DARK ORANGE** rectangle. Draw a diagonal line on the square; stitch, trim, and press. Repeat this process at the adjacent corner of the rectangle. Repeat this process at the lower corners of the rectangle using 1-inch **ORANGE/BLACK PRINT** squares.

Step 3 With right sides together, position a 1-inch **BLACK** square on the upper left corner of a 1-1/2 x 3-1/2-inch **TAN** rectangle. Draw a diagonal line on the square; stitch, trim, and press. Repeat this process at the upper right corner of the rectangle.

Make 38 fence units

Step 4 For the top/bottom picket fence border strips, sew together 8 of the Step 2 segments and 9 of the Step 3 units; press. At this point each picket fence border strip should measure 3-1/2 x 13-1/2-inches. Sew the picket fence border strips to the quilt center; press.

Step 5 For the side picket fence border strips, sew together 9 of the Step 2 segments and 10 of the Step 3 units; press. At this point each picket fence border strip should measure 3-1/2 x 15-inches. Set the side picket fence border strips aside.

Step 6 With right sides together, position a 1-inch **GREEN** square on the upper left corner of a 1-1/2 x 2-inch **BLACK** rectangle. Draw a diagonal line on the square; stitch, trim, and press. Repeat this process at the upper right corner of the rectangle.

Make 4

Step 7 With right sides together, position a 1-inch **BLACK** square on the left corner of a 1 x 1-1/2-inch **GREEN** rectangle. Draw a diagonal line on the square; stitch, trim, and press. Make 4 units. Sew a 1-1/2-inch **BLACK** square to each of the units; press.

Make 4

Step 8 Sew together the Step 6 and 7 units to make the stem units; press. Sew the stem units to the pumpkin units previously made; press. Referring to the quilt diagram on page 29, sew the pumpkin blocks to the side picket fence border strips; press. Sew the border strips to the quilt center; press.

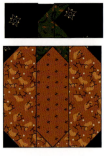

Make 4

Step 9 Attach the 2-1/2-inch wide **GREEN** outer border strips.

putting it all together

Step 1 Trim the backing and batting so they are 6-inches larger than the quilt top. Refer to **Finishing the Quilt** on page 100 for complete instructions.

Quilting Suggestions:

- **BLACK** background - small meander/stipple
- **BLACK** door - stipple
- **GREEN** roof - in-the-ditch and echo
- **GREEN** house base - channel stitch 1" apart and in-the-ditch
- Windows - use black thread and stitch "panes" in widows
- Pumpkins and star center - in-the-ditch and echo
- Star points - in-the-ditch and echo
- **BLACK** background for fence - stipple
- **BEIGE** fence - 1 line through the middle
- **GREEN** Outer border - in-the-ditch and TB 30 - 1-1/2" Beadwork

binding

Cutting

From **CHESTNUT PRINT**:
- Cut 3, 2-3/4 x 42-inch strips

Sew the binding to the quilt using a 3/8-inch seam allowance. This measurement will produce a 1/2-inch wide finished double binding. Refer to **Binding** and **Diagonal Piecing** on page 101 for complete instructions.

Trim The Tree Stocking

6 x 9-inches

Before beginning this project, read through Getting Started on page 95.

Fabrics and Supplies

1/4 yard **RED PRINT** for stocking front and back

1/4 yard **GREEN PRINT** for tree applique and stocking lining

2-inch square **GOLD PRINT** for star applique

2 x 3-inch piece **BROWN PRINT** for tree base

1/8 yard **BROWN/RED DIAGONAL PRINT** for ruffle and hanger

quilt batting, at least 9 x 24-inches

paper-backed fusible web for applique

machine embroidery thread or pearl cotton for decorative stitches: black

tear-away fabric stabilizer (optional)

template material

Trim The Tree Stocking Template

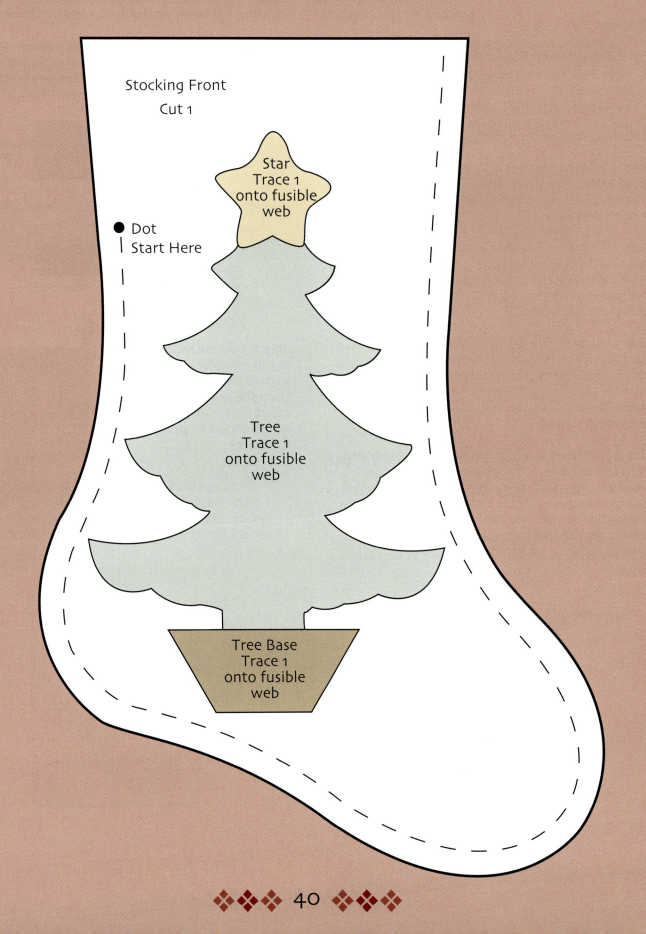

Stocking Front
Cut 1

● Dot
Start Here

Star
Trace 1
onto fusible
web

Tree
Trace 1
onto fusible
web

Tree Base
Trace 1
onto fusible
web

Pinwheel Stars

Pinwheel Stars

25-inches square

Before beginning this project, read through Getting Started on page 95.

Fabrics and Supplies

1/4 yard **ROSE DIAGONAL CHECK** for star blocks

1/4 yard **ROSE PRINT** for star blocks

1/3 yard **BEIGE PRINT** for star blocks and middle border

1/3 yard **GREEN PRINT** for star blocks and inner border

3/8 yard **FLORAL** for outer border

1/3 yard **GREEN PRINT** for binding

7/8 yard for backing

quilt batting, at least 31-inches square

Holly Lane

Holly Lane

Before beginning this project, read through Getting Started on page 95.

22 x 28-inches

Fabrics and Supplies

1/8 yard **GREEN PRINT #1** for holly sections

3/8 yard **BEIGE PRINT** for holly sections, star section, and house section

1/8 yard **RED PRINT #1** for holly sections and house section

1/8 yard **GOLD PRINT #1** for star section and windows

1/4 yard **GOLD PRINT #2** for roofs and inner border

1/8 yard **RED PRINT #2** for house section

1/8 yard **GREEN PRINT #2** for house section

1/8 yard **LIGHT GOLD PRINT** for fence section

1/8 yard **TAN PRINT** for fence section

1/4 yard **BROWN/BLACK PRINT** for middle border

1/2 yard **RED HOLLY PRINT** for outer border

1/3 yard **GREEN PRINT #3** for binding

7/8 yard for backing

quilt batting, at least 28 x 34-inches

holly section

Cutting

From **GREEN PRINT #1**:
- Cut 1, 1-7/8 x 42-inch strip
- Cut 1, 1-1/2 x 42-inch strip. From the strip cut:
   24, 1-1/2-inch squares

From **BEIGE PRINT**:
- Cut 1, 1-7/8 x 42-inch strip
- Cut 2, 1-1/2 x 42-inch strips. From the strips cut:
   16, 1-1/2 x 2-1/2-inch rectangles
   16, 1-1/2-inch squares

From **RED PRINT #1**:
- Cut 1, 1-1/2 x 42-inch strip. From the strip cut:
   8, 1-1/2-inch squares

Piecing

Step 1 With right sides together, layer the
1-7/8 x 42-inch **GREEN #1** and **BEIGE** strips. Press
together, but do not sew. Cut the layered strip into
squares. Cut the layered squares in half diagonally
to make 16 sets of triangles. Stitch 1/4-inch from the
diagonal edge of each pair of triangles; press.

Crosscut 8,
1-7/8-inch squares

Make 16, 1-1/2-inch
triangle-pieced squares

Step 2 With right sides together, position a
1-1/2-inch **GREEN #1** square on the left corner of a
1-1/2 x 2-1/2-inch **BEIGE** rectangle. Draw a diagonal
line on the square and stitch on the line. Trim the
seam allowance to 1/4-inch; press.

Make 8

Step 3 With right sides together, position a
1-1/2-inch **GREEN #1** square on the corner of a
1-1/2 x 2-1/2-inch **BEIGE** rectangle. Draw a diagonal
line on the square; stitch, trim, and press. Repeat
this process at the opposite corner of the rectangle.

Make 8

Step 4 To make a holly unit, sew together 2 of the Step 1
triangle-pieced squares, 1 of the Step 2 units, 1 of the Step 3
units, 2 of the 1-1/2-inch **BEIGE** squares, and 1 of the
1-1/2-inch **RED #1** squares. Referring to the diagram for
placement, sew the pieces together in 3 rows; press. Sew
the rows together; press. At this point each holly unit
should measure 3-1/2-inches square.

Make 8

Step 5 Sew the holly units together in 2 sections; press.
At this point each holly section should measure
3-1/2 x 12-1/2-inches.

Make 2
sections

star section

Cutting

From **GOLD PRINT #1**:
- Cut 1, 1-1/2 x 42-inch strip. From the strip cut:
   4, 1-1/2 x 3-1/2-inch rectangles
   8, 1-1/2-inch squares

From **BEIGE PRINT**:
- Cut 2, 1-1/2 x 42-inch strips. From the strips cut:
   8, 1-1/2 x 2-1/2-inch rectangles
   16, 1-1/2-inch squares

Piecing

Step 1 With right sides together, position a 1-1/2-inch
GOLD #1 square on the left corner of a 1-1/2 x 2-1/2-inch
BEIGE rectangle. Draw a diagonal line on the square;
stitch, trim, and press. Sew a 1-1/2-inch **BEIGE** square to
the left edge of the unit; press. At this point each star
point unit should measure 1-1/2 x 3-1/2-inches.

Make 8

Step 2 With right sides together, position 1-1/2-inch
BEIGE squares on the corners of a 1-1/2 x 3-1/2-inch
GOLD #1 rectangle. Draw a diagonal line on the squares;
stitch, trim, and press.

Make 4

Step 3 Sew the Step 1 star point units to the top/bottom edges of the Step 2 units; press. At this point each star unit should measure 3-1/2-inches square.

Make 4

Step 4 Sew the star units together in a row; press. At this point the star section should measure 3-1/2 x 12-1/2-inches.

Make 1 section

house section

Cutting

From **GOLD PRINT #2**:
- Cut 1, 2-1/2 x 42-inch strip. From the strip cut:
  3, 2-1/2 x 4-1/2-inch rectangles

From **BEIGE PRINT**:
- Cut 1, 2-1/2 x 42-inch strip. From the strip cut:
  6, 2-1/2-inch squares

From **RED PRINT #2**, **GREEN PRINT #2**, and **RED PRINT #1**:
- Cut 1, 1-1/2 x 42-inch strip from each fabric.
  From each strip cut:
  1, 1-1/2 x 4-1/2-inch rectangle
  6, 1-1/2-inch squares
  2, 1 x 4-1/2-inch rectangles

From **GOLD PRINT #1**:
- Cut 1, 1 x 42-inch strip. From the strip cut:
  12, 1 x 1-1/2-inch rectangles

Piecing

Step 1 With right sides together, position a 2-1/2-inch **BEIGE** square on the corner of a 2-1/2 x 4-1/2-inch **GOLD #2** rectangle. Draw a diagonal line on the square; stitch, trim, and press. Repeat this process at the opposite corner of the rectangle to make a roof unit.

Make 3

Step 2 Sew together 2 of the 1 x 1-1/2-inch **GOLD #1** rectangles and 3 of the 1-1/2-inch **RED #2** squares; press. At this point each window unit should measure 1-1/2 x 4-1/2-inches.

Make 2

Step 3 Referring to the diagram for placement, sew together the Step 2 window units, the 2, 1 x 4-1/2-inch **RED #2** rectangles, and the 1-1/2 x 4-1/2-inch **RED #2** rectangle; press. Sew a Step 1 roof unit to the top edge of this unit; press. At this point the house unit should measure 4-1/2 x 6-1/2-inches.

Make 1 **RED #2** house unit

Step 4 To make the **GREEN #2** house and the **RED #1** house, follow Steps 2 and 3 using the corresponding pieces.

Make 1 **GREEN #2** house unit   Make 1 **RED #1** house unit

Step 5 Sew the house units together in a row; press. At this point the house section should measure 6-1/2 x 12-1/2-inches.

fence section

Cutting

From **LIGHT GOLD PRINT**:
- Cut 1, 1-1/2 x 42-inch strip. From the strip cut:
  12, 1-1/2-inch squares

From **TAN PRINT**:
- Cut 1, 2-1/2 x 42-inch strip. From the strip cut:
  6, 2-1/2 x 3-1/2-inch rectangles

Piecing

Step 1 With right sides together, position a 1-1/2-inch **LIGHT GOLD** square on the upper corner of a 2-1/2 x 3-1/2-inch **TAN PRINT** rectangle. Draw a diagonal line on the square; stitch, trim, and press. Repeat this process at the adjacent corner of the rectangle to make a fence unit.

  Make 6

Step 2 Sew the fence units together in a row; press. At this point the fence section should measure 3-1/2 x 12-1/2-inches.

Quilt Center Assembly

Referring to the quilt diagram below for placement, sew together the star section, house section, and fence section; press. Sew a holly section to the top/bottom edges of the quilt center; press. At this point the quilt center should measure 12-1/2 x 18-1/2-inches.

borders

Note: *The yardage given allows for the border strips to be cut on the crosswise grain. Read through **Border** instructions on page 100 for general instructions on adding borders.*

Cutting

From **GOLD PRINT #2**:
- Cut 2 to 3, 1-1/2 x 42-inch inner border strips

From **BROWN/BLACK PRINT**:
- Cut 3, 1-1/2 x 42-inch middle border strips

From **RED HOLLY PRINT**:
- Cut 3 to 4, 3-1/2 x 42-inch outer border strips

Attaching the Borders

Step 1 Attach the 1-1/2-inch wide **GOLD #2** inner border strips.

Step 2 Attach the 1-1/2-inch wide **BROWN/BLACK** middle border strips.

Step 3 Attach the 3-1/2-inch wide **RED HOLLY PRINT** outer border strips.

putting it all together

Trim the backing and batting so they are 6-inches larger than the quilt top. Refer to **Finishing the Quilt** on page 100 for complete instructions.

Quilting Suggestions:
- The majority of the quilt was quilted in-the-ditch.
- Outer border - 1" channel stitching.

binding

Cutting

From **GREEN PRINT #3**:
- Cut 3, 2-3/4 x 42-inch strips

Sew the binding to the quilt using a 3/8-inch seam allowance. This measurement will produce a 1/2-inch wide finished double binding. Refer to **Binding** and **Diagonal Piecing** on page 101 for complete instructions.

Artificial greens and holly will last the whole season -
invert a large bowl and place a similar size bowl
on top for arrangement.

Fall Sampler

Fall Sampler

8 x 24-inches

Before beginning this project, read through Getting Started on page 95.

Fabrics and Supplies

1/8 yard **GOLD PRINT** for star center, flying geese unit, and 4-patch unit

1/8 yard **BEIGE PRINT** for background

1/8 yard **RED PRINT** for star points, flying geese unit, and 4-patch unit

1/8 yard **GREEN PRINT** for triangle-pieced squares, flying geese unit, and 4-patch unit

1/8 yard **GREEN FLORAL** for basket block, flying geese unit, and 4-patch unit

1/8 yard **DARK GOLD PRINT** for lattice strips

1/4 yard **BROWN FLORAL** for border

1/4 yard **BROWN FLORAL** for binding

3/8 yard for backing

quilt batting, at least 14 x 30-inches

star block

Makes 1 block

Cutting

From **RED PRINT**:
- Cut 1, 1-1/2 x 15-inch strip. From the strip cut:
    8, 1-1/2-inch squares

From **BEIGE PRINT**:
- Cut 1, 1-1/2 x 18-inch strip. From the strip cut:
    4, 1-1/2 x 2-1/2-inch rectangles
    4, 1-1/2-inch squares

From **GOLD PRINT**:
- Cut 1, 2-1/2-inch square

Piecing

Step 1 With right sides together, position a 1-1/2-inch **RED** square on the corner of a 1-1/2 x 2-1/2-inch **BEIGE** rectangle. Draw a diagonal line on the square and stitch on the line. Trim the seam allowance to 1/4-inch; press. Repeat this process at the opposite corner of the rectangle.

Make 4

Step 2 Sew 2 of the star point units to the top/bottom edges of the 2-1/2-inch **GOLD** square; press. Sew the 1-1/2-inch **BEIGE** squares to both ends of the remaining star point units; press. Sew the units to the side edges of the star unit; press. At this point the star block should measure 4-1/2-inches square.

Make 1

triangle-pieced squares

Makes 2 triangle-pieced squares

Cutting

From **GREEN PRINT** and **BEIGE PRINT**:
- From *each* cut 1, 2-7/8-inch square

Piecing

With right sides together, layer the 2-7/8-inch **GREEN** and **BEIGE** squares. Press together, but do not sew. Cut the layered square in half diagonally to make 2 sets of triangles. Stitch 1/4-inch from the diagonal edge of each pair of triangles; press. At this point each triangle-pieced square should measure 2-1/2-inches square. Sew the triangle-pieced squares together; press. At this point the triangle-pieced square unit should measure 2-1/2 x 4-1/2-inches.

Make 2, 2-1/2-inch triangle-pieced squares

Make 1

basket block

Makes 1 block

Cutting

From **GREEN FLORAL**:
- Cut 1, 2-7/8-inch square
- Cut 1, 2-1/2 x 4-1/2-inch rectangle
- Cut 2, 2-inch squares

From **BEIGE PRINT**:
- Cut 1, 2-7/8-inch square
- Cut 2, 2-1/2-inch squares
- Cut 2, 1-1/2-inch squares

Piecing

Step 1 With right sides together, layer the 2-7/8-inch **GREEN FLORAL** and **BEIGE** squares. Press together, but do not sew. Cut the layered square in half diagonally to make 2 sets of triangles. Stitch 1/4-inch from the diagonal edge of each pair of triangles; press.

Make 2, 2-1/2-inch triangle-pieced squares

Step 2 Position a Step 1 triangle-pieced square on the left corner of the 2-1/2 x 4-1/2-inch **GREEN FLORAL** rectangle. Draw a diagonal line on the square, stitch, trim; press. Repeat this process at the opposite corner of the rectangle. At this point the basket base should measure 2-1/2 x 4-1/2-inches.

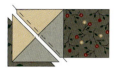 

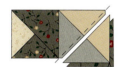 

Make 1

Step 3 To make the handle, position a 2-inch **GREEN FLORAL** square on the corner of a 2-1/2-inch **BEIGE** square. Draw a diagonal line on the **GREEN FLORAL** square, stitch, trim; press. Position a 1-1/2-inch **BEIGE** square on the corner of the unit. Draw a diagonal line on the **BEIGE** square, stitch, trim; press. Make 2 units. Sew the units together to make the handle. At this point the basket handle should measure 2-1/2 x 4-1/2-inches.

Make 2

Make 1

Step 4 Sew the basket handle to the top edge of the basket base; press. At this point the basket block should measure 4-1/2-inches square.

Make 1

flying geese units

Makes 4 units

Cutting

From **BEIGE PRINT**:
- Cut 1, 1-1/2 x 14-inch strip. From the strip cut:
  8, 1-1/2-inch squares

From **RED PRINT, GOLD PRINT, GREEN PRINT**, and **GREEN FLORAL**:
  From each cut 1, 1-1/2 x 2-1/2-inch rectangle

Piecing

Step 1 With right sides together, position a 1-1/2-inch **BEIGE** square on a corner of the 1-1/2 x 2-1/2-inch **RED** rectangle. Draw a diagonal line on the square, stitch, trim; press. Repeat this process at the opposite corner of the rectangle. Repeat with the remaining fabrics.

Make 1 **RED** unit

Make 1 **GOLD** unit   Make 1 **GREEN** unit   Make 1 **GREEN FLORAL** unit

Step 2 Sew the flying geese units together; press. At this point the flying geese unit should measure 2-1/2 x 4-1/2-inches.

Make 1

4-patch units

Makes 4 units

Cutting

From **RED PRINT, GOLD PRINT, GREEN PRINT**, and **GREEN FLORAL**:
  From each cut 1, 2-1/2-inch square

From **BEIGE PRINT**:
- Cut 8, 1-inch squares

Piecing

Step 1 Position a 1-inch **BEIGE** square on the upper right corner of the 2-1/2-inch **RED** square. Draw a diagonal line on the square, stitch, trim; press. Repeat this process at the opposite corner of the **RED** square. Repeat with the remaining fabrics.

Make 1
RED unit

Make 1
GOLD unit

Make 1
GREEN FLORAL unit

Make 1
GREEN PRINT unit

Step 2 Sew the units together in 2 rows of 2 units each. Sew the strips together; press. At this point the 4-patch block should measure 4-1/2-inches square.

Make 1

quilt center

Cutting

From **DARK GOLD PRINT**:
- Cut 1, 1-1/2 x 42-inch strip. From the strip cut:
   4, 1-1/2 x 4-1/2-inch lattice strips

Quilt Center Assembly

Refer to the quilt diagram on page 53, sew together the 1-1/2 x 4-1/2-inch **DARK GOLD** lattice strips, star block, triangle-pieced square unit, basket block, flying geese unit, and the 4-patch block; press. At this point the quilt center should measure 4-1/2 x 20-1/2-inches.

border

Note: *The yardage given allows for the border strips to be cut on the crosswise grain. Read through* **Border** *instructions on page 100 for general instructions on adding borders.*

Cutting

From **BROWN FLORAL**:
- Cut 2, 2-1/2 x 42-inch border strips

Attaching the Border

Attach the 2-1/2-inch wide **BROWN FLORAL** border strips.

putting it all together

Trim the backing and batting so they are about 6-inches larger than the quilt top. Refer to **Finishing the Quilt** on page 100 for complete instructions.

Quilting Suggestions:

- The majority of the quilt was quilted in-the-ditch.
- The outer border was quilted using a stencil with an oval design.

binding

Cutting

From **BROWN FLORAL**:
- Cut 2, 2-3/4 x 42-inch strips

Sew the binding to the quilt using a 3/8-inch seam allowance. This measurement will produce a 1/2-inch wide finished double binding. Refer to **Binding** and **Diagonal Piecing** on page 101 for complete instructions.

Picnic Stars and Checkerboard

27 x 31-inches

Before beginning this project, read through Getting Started on page 95.

Fabrics and Supplies

1/4 yard **YELLOW PRINT** for star blocks and first middle border

3/8 yard **BEIGE PRINT** for star blocks and checkerboard strips

1/3 yard **ROSE PRINT** for checkerboard strips and second middle border

1/4 yard **GREEN PRINT** for lattice strips and inner border

1/2 yard **BLUE PRINT** for outer border

1/3 yard **GREEN PRINT** for binding

1 yard for backing

quilt batting, at least 33 x 37-inches

star blocks

Makes 15 blocks

Cutting

From **YELLOW PRINT**:
- Cut 3, 1-1/2 x 42-inch strips. From the strips cut:
    15, 1-1/2 x 3-1/2-inch rectangles
    30, 1-1/2-inch squares

From **BEIGE PRINT**:
- Cut 4, 1-1/2 x 42-inch strips. From the strips cut:
    30, 1-1/2 x 2-1/2-inch rectangles
    60, 1-1/2-inch squares

Piecing

Step 1 With right sides together, position a 1-1/2-inch **YELLOW** square on the right corner of a 1-1/2 x 2-1/2-inch **BEIGE** rectangle. Draw a diagonal line on the square and stitch on the line. Trim the seam allowance to 1/4-inch; press. Sew a 1-1/2-inch **BEIGE** square to the right edge of the unit; press. At this point each unit should measure 1-1/2 x 3-1/2-inches.

Make 30

Step 2 With right sides together, position 1-1/2-inch **BEIGE** squares on both corners of a 1-1/2 x 3-1/2-inch **YELLOW** rectangle. Draw a diagonal line on the squares and stitch on the lines. Trim the seam allowance to 1/4-inch; press. At this point each unit should measure 1-1/2 x 3-1/2-inches.

Make 15

Step 3 Sew the Step 1 units to the top/bottom edges of the Step 2 units; press. At this point each star block should measure 3-1/2-inches square.

Make 15

Step 4 Sew 5 of the star blocks together to make a star block strip; press. Make a total of 3 star block strips. At this point each star block strip should measure 3-1/2 x 15-1/2-inches.

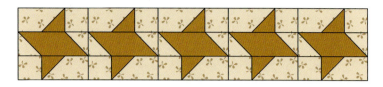

Make 3

checkerboard strips

Makes 2 strips

Cutting

From **ROSE PRINT**:
- Cut 3, 1-1/2 x 42-inch strips

From **BEIGE PRINT**:
- Cut 3, 1-1/2 x 42-inch strips

Piecing

Step 1 Aligning long raw edges, sew 1-1/2 x 42-inch **ROSE** strips to both side edges of a 1-1/2 x 42-inch **BEIGE** strip. Press the strip sets referring to **Hints and Helps for Pressing Strip Sets** on page 98. Cut the strip set into segments.

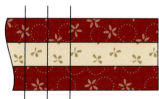

Crosscut 16, 1-1/2-inch wide segments

Step 2 Aligning long raw edges, sew 1-1/2 x 42-inch **BEIGE** strips to both side edges of a 1-1/2 x 42-inch **ROSE** strip; press. Cut the strip set into segments.

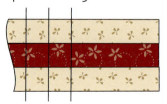

Crosscut 14, 1-1/2-inch wide segments

Step 3 Referring to the quilt diagram on page 59, sew together 8 of the Step 1 segments and 7 of the Step 2 segments; press. Make 2 checkerboard strips. At this point each checkerboard strip should measure 3-1/2 x 15-1/2-inches.

quilt center

Cutting

From **GREEN PRINT**:
- Cut 3, 1-1/2 x 42-inch strips.
  From the strips cut:
  6, 1-1/2 x 15-1/2-inch lattice and
  top/bottom inner border strips

Quilt Center Assembly

Referring to the quilt diagram on page 59
for block placement, sew together the star block
strips, checkerboard strips, and 1-1/2 x 15-1/2-inch
GREEN lattice and top/bottom inner border
strips; press. At this point the quilt center
should measure 15-1/2 x 21-1/2-inches.

borders

Note: The yardage given allows for the
border strips to be cut on the crosswise grain.
Diagonally piece the strips as needed, referring
to **Diagonal Piecing** instructions on page 101.
Read through **Border** instructions on page 100
for general instructions on adding borders.

Cutting

From **GREEN PRINT**:
- Cut 1, 1-1/2 x 42-inch side inner border
  strip. You may need to cut 1 extra strip.

From **YELLOW PRINT**:
- Cut 2, 1 x 42-inch first middle border strips

From **ROSE PRINT**:
- Cut 3, 1 x 42-inch second middle border strip.

From **BLUE PRINT**:
- Cut 3, 4-1/2 x 42-inch outer border strips

Piecing

Step 1 Attach the 1-1/2-inch wide **GREEN** side inner border
strips.

Step 2 Attach the 1-inch wide **YELLOW** first middle border
strips.

Step 3 Attach the 1-inch wide **ROSE** second middle border
strips.

Step 4 Attach the 4-1/2-inch wide **BLUE** outer border strips.

putting it all together

Trim the backing and binding so they are 6-inches larger than
the quilt top. Refer to **Finishing the Quilt** on page 100 for
complete instructions.

Quilting Suggestions:

- The majority of the quilt was quilted in the ditch.

- The outer border was channel quilted

binding

Cutting

From **GREEN PRINT**:
- Cut 3, 2-3/4 x 42-inch strips

Sew the binding to the quilt using a 3/8-inch seam allowance.
This measurement will produce a 1/2-inch wide finished
double binding. Refer to **Binding** and **Diagonal Piecing** on
page 101 for complete instructions.

It's Snowing at the Inn

It's Snowing at the Inn

36 x 40-inches

Before beginning this project, read through Getting Started on page 95.

Fabrics and Supplies

1/2 yard **LIGHT GREEN PRINT** for tree and checkerboard borders

1/8 yard **DARK GREEN PRINT** for tree

1/2 yard **BEIGE PRINT** for tree background and snowball blocks

5-inch square piece **BROWN PRINT** for tree trunk

1/2 yard **BLUE PRINT** for checkerboard borders, lattice, and inner border

3/4 yard **RED PRINT** for snowball blocks and outer border

3/8 yard **GOLD PRINT** for middle border

3/8 yard **BLUE PRINT** for binding

1-1/4 yards for backing

quilt batting, at least 42 x 46-inches

tree block

Cutting

From **LIGHT GREEN PRINT**:
- Cut 1, 3-1/2 x 42-inch strip.
  From the strip cut:
    - 2, 3-1/2-inch squares
    - 4, 2-1/2 x 4-1/2-inch rectangles
    - 4, 1-1/2-inch squares

From **DARK GREEN PRINT**:
- Cut 1, 2-1/2 x 42-inch strip.
  From the strip cut:
    - 4, 2-1/2 x 4-1/2-inch rectangles
    - 2, 2-1/2 x 3-1/2-inch rectangles
    - 6, 1-1/2-inch squares

From **BEIGE PRINT**:
- Cut 1, 3-1/2 x 42-inch strip.
  From the strip cut:
    - 2, 3-1/2 x 6-inch rectangles
    - 2, 1-1/2 x 5-inch rectangles
- Cut 2, 2-1/2 x 42-inch strips.
  From the strips cut:
    - 2, 2-1/2 x 5-inch rectangles
    - 8, 2-1/2 x 4-inch rectangles
    - 1, 1-1/2 x 11-1/2-inch rectangle

From **BROWN PRINT**:
- Cut 1, 1-1/2 x 2-1/2-inch rectangle
- Cut 2, 1-1/2-inch squares

Piecing

Step 1 With right sides together, position a 3-1/2-inch **LIGHT GREEN** square on the right corner of a 3-1/2 x 6-inch **BEIGE** rectangle. Draw a diagonal line on the square and stitch on the line. Trim the seam allowance to 1/4-inch; press. Position a 1-1/2-inch **DARK GREEN** square on the lower right corner of the unit. Draw a diagonal line on the square; stitch, trim, and press. At this point the unit should measure 3-1/2 x 6-inches.

Make 1

Step 2 With right sides together, position a 2-1/2 x 3-1/2-inch **DARK GREEN** rectangle on the right corner of a 2-1/2 x 5-inch **BEIGE** rectangle. Draw a diagonal line on the **DARK GREEN** rectangle; stitch, trim, and press. Position a 1-1/2-inch **LIGHT GREEN** square on the lower right corner of the unit. Draw a diagonal line on the square; stitch, trim, and press. At this point the unit should measure 2-1/2 x 6-inches.

Make 1

Step 3 With right sides together, position a 2-1/2 x 4-1/2-inch **LIGHT GREEN** rectangle on the right corner of a 2-1/2 x 4-inch **BEIGE** rectangle. Draw a diagonal line on the **LIGHT GREEN** rectangle; stitch, trim, and press. Position a 1-1/2-inch **DARK GREEN** square on the lower right corner of the unit. Draw a diagonal line on the square; stitch, trim, and press. At this point each unit should measure 2-1/2 x 6-inches.

Make 2

Step 4 With right sides together, position a 2-1/2 x 4-1/2-inch **DARK GREEN** rectangle on the right corner of a 2-1/2 x 4-inch **BEIGE** rectangle. Draw a diagonal line on the **DARK GREEN** rectangle; stitch, trim, and press. Make 2 units. For 1 of the units, position a 1-1/2-inch **LIGHT GREEN** square on the lower right corner of the unit. Draw a diagonal line on the square; stitch, trim, and press. For the remaining unit, position a 1-1/2-inch **BROWN** square on the lower right corner of the unit. Draw a diagonal line on the square; stitch, trim, and press. At this point each unit should measure 2-1/2 x 6-inches.

Make 1

Make 1

Step 5 Referring to the diagram, sew together the Step 1, 2, 3, and 4 units. Press all the seam allowances toward the top of the tree. At this point the left tree unit should measure 6 x 13-1/2-inches.

Make 1

Step 6 With right sides together, position a 3-1/2-inch **LIGHT GREEN** square on the left corner of a 3-1/2 x 6-inch **BEIGE** rectangle. Draw a diagonal line on the square; stitch, trim, and press. Position a 1-1/2-inch **DARK GREEN** square on the lower left corner of the unit. Draw a diagonal line on the square; stitch, trim, and press. At this point the unit should measure 3-1/2 x 6-inches.

Make 1

Step 7 With right sides together, position a 2-1/2 x 3-1/2-inch **DARK GREEN** rectangle on the left corner of a 2-1/2 x 5-inch **BEIGE** rectangle. Draw a diagonal line on the **DARK GREEN** rectangle; stitch, trim, and press. Position a 1-1/2-inch **LIGHT GREEN** square on the lower left corner of the unit. Draw a diagonal line on the square; stitch, trim, and press. At this point the unit should measure 2-1/2 x 6-inches.

Make 1

Step 8 With right sides together, position a 2-1/2 x 4-1/2-inch **LIGHT GREEN** rectangle on the left corner of a 2-1/2 x 4-inch **BEIGE** rectangle. Draw a diagonal line on the **LIGHT GREEN** rectangle; stitch, trim, and press. Position a 1-1/2-inch **DARK GREEN** square on the lower left corner of the unit. Draw a diagonal line on the square; stitch, trim, and press. At this point each unit should measure 2-1/2 x 6-inches.

Make 2

Step 9 With right sides together, position a 2-1/2 x 4-1/2-inch **DARK GREEN** rectangle on the left corner of a 2-1/2 x 4-inch **BEIGE** rectangle. Draw a diagonal line on the **DARK GREEN** rectangle; stitch, trim, and press. Make 2 units. For 1 of the units, position a 1-1/2-inch **LIGHT GREEN** square on the lower left corner of the unit. Draw a diagonal line on the square; stitch, trim, and press. For the remaining unit, position a 1-1/2-inch **BROWN** square on the lower left corner of the unit. Draw a diagonal line on the square; stitch, trim, and press. At this point each unit should measure 2-1/2 x 6-inches.

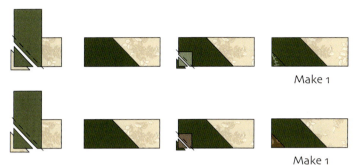

Make 1

Make 1

Step 10 Referring to the diagram, sew together the Step 6, 7, 8, and 9 units. Press all the seam allowances toward the bottom of the tree. At this point the right tree unit should measure 6 x 13-1/2-inches.

Make 1

Step 11 Referring to the tree block diagram, sew together the Step 5 and Step 10 tree units to make the tree unit; press. At this point the tree unit should measure 11-1/2 x 13-1/2-inches.

Step 12 Sew the 1-1/2 x 5-inch **BEIGE** rectangles to both side edges of the 1-1/2 x 2-1/2-inch **BROWN** rectangle; press. Sew this unit to the bottom edge of the tree unit; press. Sew the 1-1/2 x 11-1/2-inch **BEIGE** rectangle to the top edge of the tree unit; press. At this point the tree block should measure 11-1/2 x 15-1/2-inches.

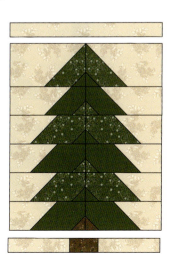

Make 1

A Tisket,
A Tasket,
A Little Basket

17 x 23-inches

Before beginning this project, read through Getting Started on page 95.

Fabrics and Supplies

6" x 12" rectangle *each* of **8 COORDINATING PRINTS** for baskets

1/2 yard **BEIGE PRINT** for background and side and corner triangles

1/4 yard **GREEN PRINT** for inner border and corner squares

1/4 yard **FLORAL** for outer border

1/4 yard **GOLD DIAGONAL PRINT** for binding

5/8 yard for backing

quilt batting, at least 23 x 29-inches

basket blocks

Makes 8 blocks

Cutting

From **each** of the **8 COORDINATING PRINTS**:
- Cut 1, 4-7/8-inch square.
  Cut the square in half diagonally to make 2 triangles. You will be using only 1 triangle for the basket base.
- Cut 1, 1-3/8 x 6-1/2-inch **bias** strip for each basket handle

From **BEIGE PRINT**:
- Cut 1, 4-7/8 x 42-inch strip.
  From the strip cut:
  4, 4-7/8-inch squares.
  Cut the squares in half diagonally to make 8 applique foundation triangles.

Prepare the Basket Handle Appliques

Step 1 To make a basket handle, fold a **PRINT** 1-3/8 x 6-1/2-inch strip in half lengthwise with wrong sides together; press. To keep the raw edges aligned, stitch a scant 1/4-inch away from the edges. Fold the strip in half again so the raw edges are hidden by the first folded edge; press. Hand-baste if needed.

Step 2 Referring to the handle placement diagram on page 71, position the prepared basket handle on a beige applique foundation triangle and hand-baste or pin in place. Hand applique the basket handles in place. Repeat to make 8 handle units.

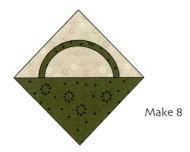

Make 8

Step 3 Sew the corresponding **PRINT** triangle to the bottom edge of each handle unit; press. Repeat to make 8 basket units.

quilt center

Note: The side and corner triangles are larger than necessary and will be trimmed before the borders are added.

Side triangles

Cutting

From **BEIGE PRINT**:
- Cut 1, 7-1/2 x 42-inch strip.
  From the strip cut:
  2, 7-1/2-inch squares.
  Cut the squares diagonally into quarters to make 8 triangles. You will be using only 6 side triangles. Also cut 2, 4-1/2-inch squares. Cut the squares in half diagonally to make 4 corner squares.

Corner triangles

Quilt Center Assembly

Step 1 Referring to the quilt center assembly diagram, sew together the basket blocks and side triangles in 4 diagonal rows. Press the seam allowances in alternating directions by rows so the seams will fit snugly together with less bulk.

Step 2 Pin the block rows together, sew and press. Sew the corner triangles to the quilt center; press.

Step 3 Trim away the excess fabric from the side and corner triangles taking care to allow a 1/4-inch seam allowance beyond the corners of each block. Refer to **Trimming Side and Corner Triangles** on page 98 for complete instructions.

Quilt Center Assembly

borders

Note: *The yardage given allows for the border strips to be cut on the crosswise grain. Read through **Border** instructions on page 100 for general instructions on adding borders.*

Cutting

From **GREEN PRINT**:
- Cut 2, 1-1/2 x 42-inch inner border strips
- Cut 4, 2-1/2-inch corner squares

From **FLORAL**:
- Cut 2, 2-1/2 x 42-inch outer border strips

Attaching the Borders

Step 1 Attach the 1-1/2-inch wide **GREEN** inner border strips.

Step 2 Attach the 2-1/2-inch wide **FLORAL** top/bottom outer border strips; press.

Step 3 For the side borders, measure just the quilt top including seam allowances, but not the top/bottom borders just added. Cut the 2-1/2-inch wide **FLORAL** side outer border strips to this length. Sew a 2-1/2-inch **GREEN** corner square to both ends of the border strips; press. Sew the border strips to the side edges of the quilt center; press.

putting it all together

Trim the backing and batting so they are 6-inches larger than the quilt top. Refer to **Finishing the Quilt** on page 100 for complete instructions.

Quilting Suggestions:
- Baskets - echo and in-the-ditch.
- **BEIGE** background - echo.
- **GREEN** border - in-the-ditch.
- Outer border - **TB 30 - 1-1/2" Beadwork.**

binding

Cutting

From **GOLD DIAGONAL PRINT**:
- Cut 2, 2-3/4-inch wide bias strips

Sew the binding to the quilt using a 3/8-inch seam allowance. This measurement will produce a 1/2-inch wide finished double binding. Refer to **Binding** and **Diagonal Piecing** on page 101 for complete instructions.

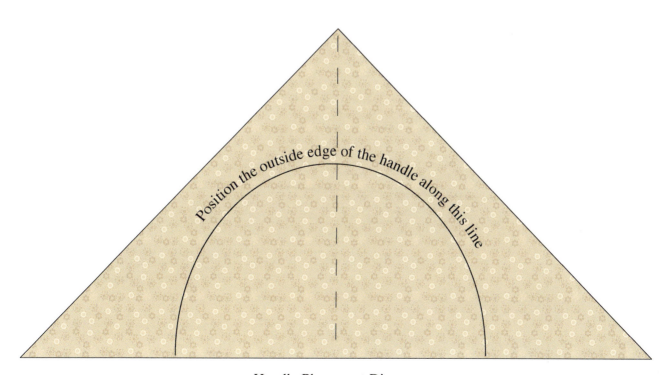

Position the outside edge of the handle along this line

Handle Placement Diagram

Cabin Maples

Cabin Maples

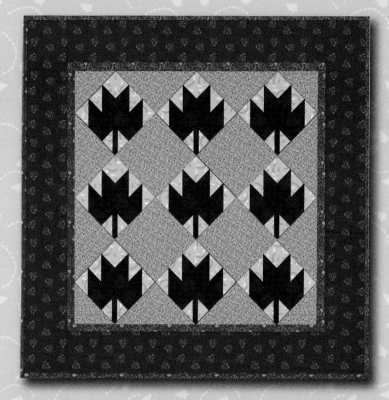

27-inches square

Before beginning this project, read through Getting Started on page 95.

Fabrics and Supplies

1/3 yard **RUST PRINT** for leaf blocks

1/3 yard **BEIGE PRINT** for leaf blocks

1/2 yard **GOLD PRINT** for alternate blocks and side and corner triangles

1/8 yard **GREEN PRINT** for inner border

1/2 yard **BROWN PRINT** for outer border

1/3 yard **GREEN PRINT** for binding

1 yard for backing

quilt batting, at least 33-inches square

leaf blocks

Makes 9 blocks

Cutting

From **RUST PRINT**:
- Cut 1, 2-3/8 x 42-inch strip
- Cut 2, 2 x 42-inch strips. From the strips cut:
    9, 2 x 5-inch rectangles
    9, 2 x 3-1/2-inch rectangles
- Cut 1, 1 x 42-inch strip. From the strip cut:
    9, 1 x 3-inch strips

From **BEIGE PRINT**:
- Cut 1, 2-3/8 x 42-inch strip
- Cut 2, 2 x 42-inch strips. From the strips cut:
    27, 2-inch squares
- Cut 1 more 2 x 42-inch strip. From the strip cut:
    9, 2-inch squares. Cut the squares in half diagonally to make 18 triangles.

Piecing

Step 1 With right sides together, layer the 2-3/8-inch wide **RUST** and **BEIGE PRINT** strips in pairs. Press together, but do not sew. Cut the layered strip into squares. Cut the layered squares in half diagonally to make 18 sets of triangles. Stitch 1/4-inch from the diagonal edge of each pair of triangles, and press. At this point each triangle-pieced square should measure 2-inches square.

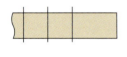

Crosscut 9, 2-3/8-inch squares

Make 18, 2-inch triangle-pieced squares

Step 2 Sew the triangle-pieced squares together in pairs and press. Sew a 2-inch **BEIGE PRINT** square to the right edge of the triangle-pieced square unit. At this point each section should measure 2 x 5-inches.

Make 9

Step 3 Position a 2-inch **BEIGE PRINT** square on the corner of a 2 x 5-inch **RUST** rectangle. Draw a diagonal line on the square and stitch on the line. Trim the seam allowances to 1/4-inch and press. At this point each section should measure 2 x 5-inches.

Make 9

Step 4 Position a 2-inch **BEIGE PRINT** square on the corner of a 2 x 3-1/2-inch **RUST** rectangle. Draw a diagonal line on the square and stitch on the line. Trim the seam allowance to 1/4-inch and press.

Make 9

Step 5 To make a stem unit, center a **BEIGE PRINT** triangle on a 1 x 3-inch **RUST** strip and stitch a 1/4-inch seam. Center another **BEIGE PRINT** triangle on the opposite edge of the **RUST** strip and stitch. Press the seam allowance toward the **RUST** strip. Trim the stem unit so it measures 2-inches square.

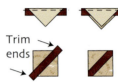

Trim ends

Make 9 stem units

Step 6 Sew the stem unit to the left edge of the Step 4 unit and press. At this point each section should measure 2 x 5-inches.

Make 9

Step 7 Referring to the block diagram, sew the Step 2, 3, and 6 sections together and press. At this point each leaf block should measure 5-inches square.

Step 2
Step 3
Step 6

Make 9

quilt center

Note: The side and corner triangles are larger than necessary and will be trimmed before the borders are added.

Cutting

From **GOLD PRINT**:
- Cut 1, 9 x 42-inch strip.
    From the strip cut:
    2, 9-inch squares. Cut the squares diagonally into quarters for a total of 8 triangles.
- Cut 1, 5 x 42-inch strip.
    From the strip cut:
    4, 5-inch alternate block squares. Also, cut 2, 5-inch squares. Cut the squares in half diagonally for a total of 4 corner triangles.

side triangles

corner triangles

Quilt Center Assembly

Step 1 Referring to the **Quilt Center Assembly** diagram for block placement, sew the leaf blocks, alternate blocks, and **GOLD** side triangles together in diagonal rows to make 5 block rows. Press the seam allowances toward the alternate blocks and side triangles.

Step 2 Pin the rows at the block intersections and sew the rows together. Press the seam allowances in one direction.

Step 3 Sew the **GOLD** corner triangles to the quilt center; press.

Step 4 Trim away the excess fabric from the side and corner triangles taking care to allow a 1/4-inch seam allowance beyond the corners of each block. Refer to **Trimming Side and Corner Triangles** on page 98 for complete instructions.

Quilt Center Assembly

borders

Note: The yardage given allows for the border strips to be cut on the crosswise grain. Read through *Border* instructions on page 100 for general instructions on adding borders.

Cutting

From **GREEN PRINT**:
- Cut 2, 1 x 42-inch inner border strips

From **BROWN PRINT**:
- Cut 3, 4 x 42-inch outer border strips

Attaching the Borders

Step 1 Attach the 1-inch wide **GREEN** inner border.

Step 2 Attach the 4-inch wide **BROWN** outer border.

putting it all together

Trim the backing and batting so they are 6-inches larger than the quilt top. Refer to **Finishing the Quilt** on page 100 for complete instructions.

Quilting Suggestions:

- Leaf blocks - in-the-ditch and quilting lines in leaves.
- Alternate blocks - TB 56 - 3-1/2" Ice Crystal.
- Side triangles - 1/2 of TB 56 - 3-1/2" Ice Crystal.
- Corner triangles - 1/4 of TB 56 - 3-1/2" Ice Crystal.
- **GREEN** inner border - in-the-ditch
- **BROWN** outer border - crosshatch

binding

Cutting

From **GREEN GRID**:
- Cut 3, 2-3/4 x 42-inch strips

Sew the binding to the quilt using a 3/8-inch seam allowance. This measurement will produce a 1/2-inch wide finished double binding. Refer to page 101 for **Binding** and **Diagonal Piecing** instructions.

Goose Chase

Goose Chase

22-inches square

Before beginning this project, read through Getting Started on page 95.

Fabrics and Supplies

1/4 yard **ROSE DIAGONAL PRINT** for blocks

1/4 yard **BEIGE PRINT #1** for block and pieced border

1/4 yard **BEIGE PRINT #2** for block and pieced border

1/4 yard **BEIGE PRINT #3** for block and pieced border

1/8 yard **BLUE PRINT** for inner border

1/4 yard **GOLD PRINT** for center square, and corner squares

1/3 yard **YELLOW FLORAL** for outer border

3/8 yard **ROSE DIAGONAL PRINT** for binding

7/8 yard for backing

quilt batting, at least 28-inches square

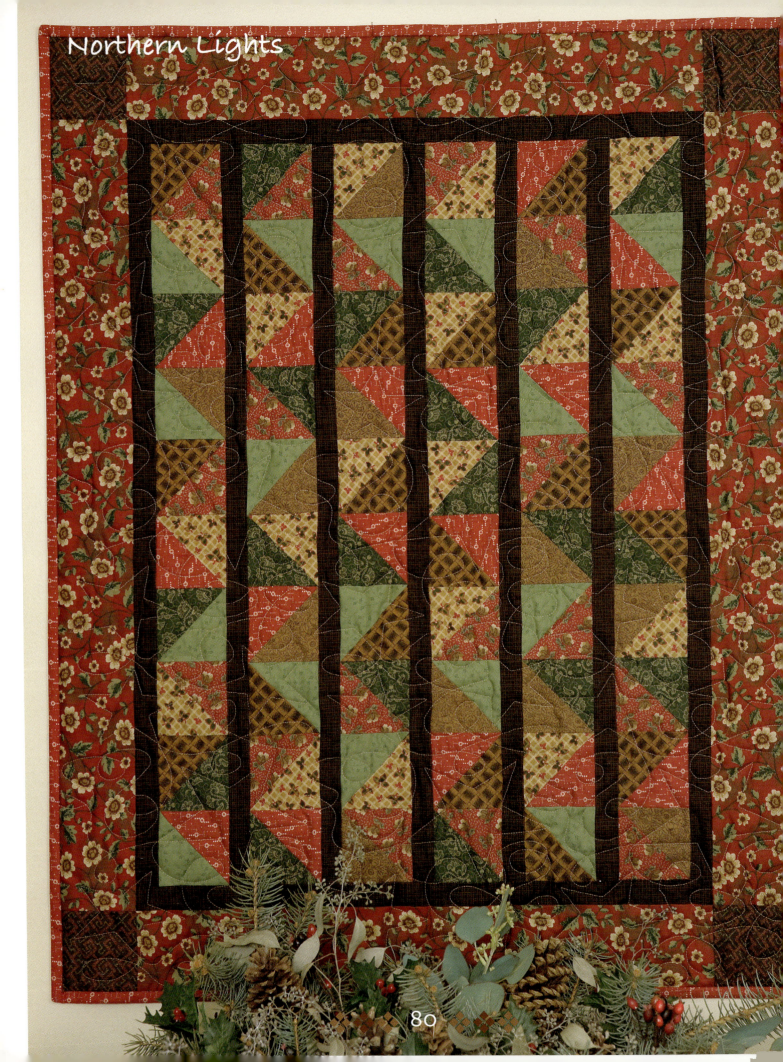

Northern Lights

32 x 39-inches

Before beginning this project, read through Getting Started on page 95.

Fabrics and Supplies

1/4 yard *each* of **7 COORDINATING PRINTS** for triangle-pieced squares

1/2 yard **BROWN/BLACK PRINT** for lattice and inner border

5/8 yard **RED FLORAL** for outer border

1/4 yard **BROWN/RED PRINT** for corner squares

1/2 yard **RED PRINT** for binding

1-1/4 yards for backing

quilt batting, at least 38 x 45-inches

triangle-pieced square blocks

Makes 60 blocks

Cutting

From **each** of the **7 COORDINATING PRINTS**:
- Cut 1, 3-7/8-inch x 42-inch strip. From each strip cut: at least 10, 3-7/8-inch squares. Cut the squares in half diagonally to make approximately 140 triangles. You will have extra triangles to mix and match to get the look you want.

Piecing

Step 1 With right sides together, randomly sew together the triangles in pairs to make 60, 3-1/2-inch triangle-pieced squares; press.

Make 60, 3-1/2-inch triangle-pieced squares

Step 2 Sew the triangle-pieced squares together in 6 vertical rows with 10 triangle-pieced squares in each row; press. Referring to the quilt diagram on page 81, alternate the direction of the angles; press. At this point each block row should measure 3-1/2 x 30-1/2-inches.

quilt center and inner border

*Note: Read through **Border** instructions on page 100 for general instructions on adding borders.*

Cutting

From BROWN/BLACK PRINT:
- Cut 9, 1-1/2 x 42-inch lattice strips/inner border strips

Quilt Center Assembly

Step 1 Cut 7 of the 1-1/2-inch wide **BROWN/BLACK** lattice strips/side inner border strips to 30-1/2-inches long (or the length of your block rows).

Step 2 Pin and sew together the 6 block rows and the 7 lattice strips/side inner border strips; press.

Step 3 Measure the quilt from left to right through the center to determine the length of the top/bottom inner borders. Cut 2 of the 1-1/2-inch wide **BROWN/BLACK** top/bottom inner border strips to this length. Sew the strips to the top/bottom edge of the quilt; press. At this point the quilt center should measure 25-1/2 x 32-1/2-inches.

outer border

*Note: The yardage given allows for the outer border strips to be cut on the lengthwise grain. Read through **Border** instructions on page 100 for general instructions on adding borders.*

Cutting

From **RED FLORAL**:
- Cut 4, 4 x 42-inch outer border strips

From **BROWN/RED PRINT**:
- Cut 1, 4 x 42-inch strip. From the strip cut: 4, 4-inch corner squares

Attaching the Border

Step 1 Attach the 4-inch wide **RED FLORAL** top/bottom outer border strips. Trim the strips as needed.

Step 2 For the side outer borders, measure the quilt from top to bottom, including the seam allowances but not the borders just added. Trim the 4 x 42-inch **RED FLORAL** outer border strips to this length. Sew the 4-inch **BROWN/RED** corner squares to both ends of the side border strips; press. Sew the border strips to the side edges of the quilt; press.

putting it all together

Trim the backing and batting so they are 6-inches larger than the quilt top. Refer to **Finishing the Quilt** on page 100 for complete instructions. Our quilt was machine quilted with an allover quilt design.

binding

Cutting

From **RED PRINT**:
- Cut 4, 2-3/4 x 42-inch strips

Sew the binding to the quilt using a 3/8-inch seam allowance. This measurement will produce a 1/2-inch wide finished double binding. Refer to **Binding** and **Diagonal Piecing** on page 101 for complete instructions.

A house becomes a home
when it reflects the interests
of the people living within.

Daisy Bouquet

Daisy Bouquet

26-inches square

Before beginning this project, read through Getting Started on page 95.

Fabrics and Supplies

1/8 yard each of 4 assorted **BLUE PRINTS** for Log Cabin strips

1/8 yard each of 4 assorted **RED PRINTS** for Log Cabin strips

1/4 yard **DARK GOLD PRINT** for Log Cabin center squares and middle border

1/4 yard **RED PRINT #1** for lattice and inner border

3/8 yard **BLUE PRINT** for outer border

1/8 yard **LIGHT GOLD PRINT** for petal appliques

1/8 yard **MEDIUM GOLD PRINT** for petal appliques

7-inch square **RED PRINT #2** for flower center appliques

1/8 yard **GREEN PRINT** for stem and leaf appliques

1/3 yard **BLUE PRINT** for binding

1 yard for backing

1 spool of fine invisible polyester thread

lightweight cardboard for circular appliques

quilt batting, at least 32-inches square

log cabin blocks

Makes 4 blocks

Cutting

From each of the 4 assorted **BLUE PRINTS**:
*   Cut 2, 1-1/4 x 42-inch strips

From each of the 4 assorted **RED PRINTS**:
*   Cut 2, 1-1/4 x 42-inch strips

From **DARK GOLD PRINT**:
*   Cut 4, 2-inch center squares

From **RED PRINT#1**:
*   Cut 1, 1-1/2 x 42-inch strip. From this strip cut:
        1, 1-1/2 x 16-1/2-inch lattice strip
        2, 1-1/2 x 8-inch lattice strips

Piecing

Step 1   Make 4 Log Cabin blocks. To do so, sew a 1-1/4 x 42-inch assorted **BLUE** strip to a 2-inch **DARK GOLD PRINT** center square and press. Then trim the strip even with the edges of the center square, creating a two-piece unit.

Step 2   Continue adding the 1-1/4-inch wide assorted **BLUE** and **RED** strips to the center square in a counterclockwise direction. There should be 4 strips on all sides of the **DARK GOLD PRINT** center square. At this point each block should measure 8-inches square.

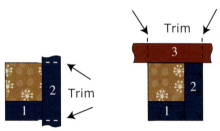

Step 3   Sew a Log Cabin block to both sides of a 1-1/2 x 8-inch **RED PRINT #1** lattice strip and press. Repeat for remaining 2 blocks. Sew a block row to both sides of the 1-1/2 x 16-1/2-inch **RED PRINT #1** lattice strip and press. At this point the quilt center should measure 16-1/2-inches square.

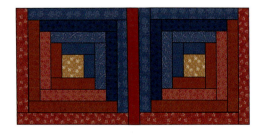

Make 2

borders

*Note: The yardage given allows for the border strips to be cut on the crosswise grain. Read through **Border** instructions on page 100 for general instructions on adding borders.*

Cutting

From **RED PRINT #1**:
*   Cut 2, 1-1/2 x 42-inch inner border strips

From **DARK GOLD PRINT**:
*   Cut 2, 1-1/2 x 42-inch middle border strips

From **BLUE PRINT**:
*   Cut 3, 3-1/2 x 42-inch outer border strips

Attaching the Borders

Step 1   Attach the 1-1/2-inch wide **RED PRINT #1** inner border strips.

Step 2   Attach the 1-1/2-inch wide **DARK GOLD PRINT** middle border strips.

Step 3   Attach the 3-1/2-inch wide **BLUE PRINT** outer border strips.

flower applique

Cutting

From **LIGHT GOLD PRINT**:
*   Cut 20 of Petal A for flower petals

From **MEDIUM GOLD PRINT**:
*   Cut 20 of Petal A for flower petals

Assembling the Flowers

Step 1   Fold the **LIGHT GOLD** and **MEDIUM GOLD** A pieces in half lengthwise, right sides together. Sew a 1/4-inch seam along the top edge. Clip off the excess seam allowance of the point. Turn right side out. Push the tip out with a blunt pencil. Press, making sure the seam line goes down the center so that both sides are equal.

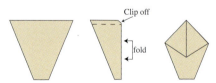

Step 2   To make each flower, with right side together, sew 4 **LIGHT GOLD PRINT** petals and 4 **MEDIUM GOLD** petals together, alternating colors. Start sewing at the upper edge of the petals. You will have a hole in the center of the flower which will be covered by the flower center applique. Press seam allowances in one direction. Make 5 flowers.

flower center cardboard appliqué method

Step 1 Make a cardboard template using the Flower Center B pattern.

Step 2 Position the flower center B template on the wrong side of the fabric chosen for the appliqué and trace around the template 5 times, leaving a 1/2-inch margin around each shape. Remove the template and cut a scant 1/4-inch beyond the drawn lines.

Step 3 To create smooth, round circles, run a line of basting stitches around each circle, placing the stitches halfway between the drawn line and the cut edge of the circle. After basting, keep the needle and thread attached for the next step.

Make 5 **RED PRINT #2** flower centers

Step 4 Place the cardboard template on the wrong side of the fabric circle and tug on the basting stitches, gathering the fabric over the template. When the thread is tight, space the gathers evenly, and make a knot to secure the thread. Clip the thread, press the circle, and remove the cardboard template.

Step 5 Appliqué the flower center to the flower with matching thread. Continue this process to add the remaining flower centers to the flowers.

Step 6 The flowers will be appliquéd to the quilt after the stems and leaves are appliquéd.

stem and leaf appliqué

Cutting

From **GREEN PRINT**:
- Cut 4, 1-1/2 x 8-inch strips for stems
- Cut 8, of Leaf C for leaves

Prepare the Stems and Leaves

Step 1 To make the **GREEN** stems (see cut sizes above), fold in the long edges, wrong sides together, to meet at the center. The stems should measure 1-1/2 x 8-inches.

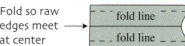

Fold so raw edges meet at center

Make 4 stems

Step 2 Referring to the quilt diagram, position the stems on the quilt and pin in place. Each stem should run diagonally through each block and should be about 2-inches apart at the center. Position a flower at the center to make sure it covers the raw edges of the stems, adjust the stems if necessary.

Step 3 Fold the **GREEN** C leaves in half lengthwise, right sides together. Sew a 1/4-inch seam along the top edge. Clip off the excess seam allowance of the point.

Step 4 Turn right side out. Push tip out with a blunt pencil. Press, making sure the seam line goes down the center so that both side are equal. Fold the long edges under 3/8-inch to the wrong sides, and press.

Clip off / Fold

Step 5 Referring to the diagram, position the leaves in place on the quilt top, tucking the bottom raw edges under the long stems. Pin the leaves in place.

putting it all together

Trim the backing and batting so they are 6-inches larger than the quilt top. Refer to **Finishing the Quilt** on page 100 for complete instructions. Our quilt was machine quilted with a meander design.

binding

Cutting

From **BLUE PRINT**:
- Cut 3, 2-3/4 x 42-inch strips

Sew the binding to the quilt using a 3/8-inch seam allowance. This measurement will produce a 1/2-inch wide finished double binding. Refer to page 101 for **Binding** and **Diagonal Piecing** Instructions.

Daisy Bouquet Templates

Flower Center B
Trace 1 onto lightweight cardboard
Make 5 RED PRINT #2

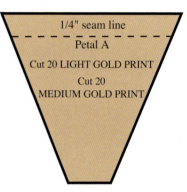

1/4" seam line
Petal A
Cut 20 LIGHT GOLD PRINT
Cut 20 MEDIUM GOLD PRINT

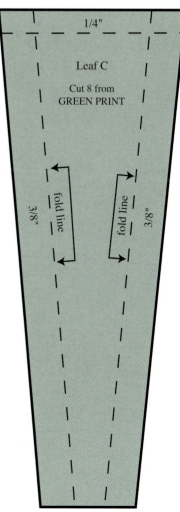

1/4"
Leaf C
Cut 8 from GREEN PRINT
3/8"   fold line   fold line   3/8"

Harvest Pumpkins

Harvest Pumpkins

26-inches square

Before beginning this project, read through Getting Started on page 95.

Fabrics and Supplies

5/8 yard **GREEN PRINT** for leaf blocks and outer border

1/2 yard **BEIGE PRINT** for background and middle border

1/4 yard **DARK GOLD PRINT** for leaf blocks

1/8 yard **ORANGE PRINT** for pumpkin blocks

1/4 yard **RUST PRINT** for pumpkin blocks

1/8 yard **BLACK PRINT** for pumpkin stems and inner border

3/8 yard **BLACK PRINT** for binding

1 yard for backing

quilt batting, at least 32-inches square

leaf blocks

Makes 6 green leaf units
Makes 6 dark gold leaf units

Cutting

From **GREEN PRINT**:
- Cut 1, 2-7/8 x 42-inch strip. From the strip cut:
  3, 2-7/8-inch squares. Cut the squares
  diagonally in half to make 6 triangles.
  Also cut 6, 3/4 x 2-1/2-inch stem rectangles
- Cut 1, 1-1/2 x 42-inch strip. From the strip cut:
  12, 1-1/2 x 2-1/2-inch rectangles
  6, 1-1/2-inch squares

From **BEIGE PRINT**:
- Cut 1, 3-1/2 x 42-inch strip. From the strip cut:
  8, 3-1/2-inch squares
- Cut 1, 1-7/8 x 42-inch strip. From the strip cut:
  12, 1-7/8-inch squares. Cut the squares
  diagonally in half to make 24 triangles.
- Cut 1, 1-5/8 x 42-inch strip. From the strip cut:
  12, 1-5/8-inch squares
- Cut 1, 1-1/2 x 42-inch strip. From the strip cut:
  24, 1-1/2-inch squares

From **DARK GOLD**:
- Cut 1, 2-7/8 x 42-inch strip. From the strip cut:
  3, 2-7/8-inch squares. Cut the squares
  diagonally in half to make 6 triangles.
  Also cut 6, 3/4 x 2-1/2-inch stem rectangles
- Cut 1, 1-1/2 x 42-inch strip. From the strip cut:
  12, 1-1/2 x 2-1/2-inch rectangles
  6, 1-1/2-inch squares

Piecing

Step 1 Sew 2 of the **BEIGE** triangles to both side
edges of a 1-1/2-inch **GREEN** square; press. Sew a
GREEN triangle to the edge of the unit; press.
At this point each unit should measure
2-1/2-inches square.

  Make 6

Step 2 With right sides together, position a
1-1/2-inch **BEIGE** square on the right corner of
a 1-1/2 x 2-1/2-inch **GREEN** rectangle. Draw a
diagonal line on the square and stitch on the line.
Trim the seam allowance to 1/4-inch; press.

  Make 6

Step 3 With right sides together, position a 1-1/2-inch **BEIGE**
square on the left corner of a 1-1/2 x 2-1/2-inch **GREEN** rectangle.
Draw a diagonal line on the square; stitch, trim, and press.

  Make 6

Step 4 To make the stem unit, cut a 1-5/8-inch **BEIGE** square in
half diagonally. Center a **BEIGE** triangle on a 3/4 x 2-1/2-inch
GREEN rectangle; stitch. Center another **BEIGE** triangle on the
opposite edge of the **GREEN** rectangle; stitch and press. Trim the
stem unit so it measures 1-1/2-inches square. Sew the stem unit
to the left edge of the Step 2 leaf unit; press. At this point the
unit should measure 1-1/2 x 3-1/2-inches.

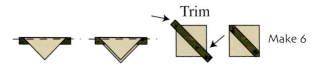 Trim   Make 6

 Make 6

Step 5 Sew the Step 1 unit to the right edge of
the Step 3 unit; press. Sew the Step 4 unit to the
top edge of the unit; press. At this point each
leaf unit should measure 3-1/2-inches square.

Make 6 **GREEN**
leaf units

Step 6 Sew 2 of the **BEIGE** triangles to both side edges of a
1-1/2-inch **DARK GOLD** square; press. Sew a **DARK GOLD**
triangle to the edge of the unit; press.

  Make 6

Step 7 With right sides together, position a 1-1/2-inch **BEIGE**
square on the right corner of a 1-1/2 x 2-1/2-inch **DARK GOLD**
rectangle. Draw a diagonal line on the square; stitch, trim, and
press.

  Make 6

Step 8 With right sides together, position a 1-1/2-inch **BEIGE**
square on the left corner of a 1-1/2 x 2-1/2-inch **DARK GOLD**
rectangle. Draw a diagonal line on the square; stitch, trim, and
press.

  Make 6

Step 9 To make the stem unit, cut a 1-5/8-inch **BEIGE** square in half diagonally. Center a **BEIGE** triangle on a 3/4 x 2-1/2-inch **DARK GOLD** rectangle; stitch. Center another **BEIGE** triangle on the opposite edge of the **DARK GOLD** rectangle; stitch and press. Trim the stem unit. Sew the stem unit to the left edge of the Step 7 leaf unit; press.

Trim

Make 6

Make 6

Step 10 Sew the Step 6 unit to the right edge of the Step 8 unit; press. Sew the Step 9 unit to the top edge of the unit; press. At this point each leaf unit should measure 3-1/2-inches square.

Make 6 **DARK GOLD** leaf units

Step 11 Referring to the diagram, sew a Step 5 and a Step 10 leaf unit together; press. Make 2 units. Sew the units together to make a block; press. At this point the block should measure 6-1/2-inches square.

Make 2

Make 1

Step 12 Referring to the diagram, sew a Step 5 **GREEN** leaf unit to the left edge of a 3-1/2-inch **BEIGE** square; press.

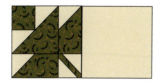

Make 4

Step 13 Referring to the diagram, sew a Step 10 **DARK GOLD** leaf unit to the right edge of a 3-1/2-inch **BEIGE** square; press.

Make 4

Step 14 Sew the Step 12 and Step 13 units together to make a block; press. At this point each block should measure 6-1/2-inches square.

Make 4

pumpkin blocks

Makes 4 blocks

Cutting

From **ORANGE PRINT**:
- Cut 2, 1-1/2 x 42-inch strips.
  From the strips cut:
  8, 1-1/2 x 5-1/2-inch rectangles
  16, 1-1/2-inch squares

From **RUST PRINT**:
- Cut 1, 2-1/2 x 42-inch strip.
  From the strip cut:
  4, 2-1/2 x 5-1/2-inch rectangles
- Cut 2, 1-1/2 x 42-inch strips.
  From the strips cut:
  8, 1-1/2 x 5-1/2-inch rectangles
  16, 1-1/2-inch squares

From **BEIGE PRINT**:
- Cut 2, 1-1/2 x 42-inch strips.
  From the strips cut:
  8, 1-1/2 x 2-1/2-inch rectangles
  24, 1-1/2-inch squares

From **BLACK PRINT**:
- Cut 1, 1-1/2 x 42-inch strip.
  From the strip cut:
  4, 1-1/2 x 2-1/2-inch rectangles

Piecing

Step 1 With right sides together, position 1-1/2-inch **ORANGE** squares on 2 opposite corners of a 2-1/2 x 5-1/2-inch **RUST** rectangle. Draw a diagonal line on the squares; stitch, trim, and press. Repeat this process on the opposite corners of the rectangle.

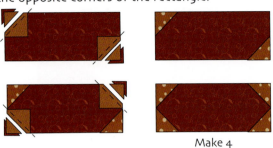

Make 4

Step 2 With right sides together, position 1-1/2-inch **RUST** squares on the corners of a 1-1/2 x 5-1/2-inch **ORANGE** rectangle. Draw a diagonal line on the squares; stitch, trim, and press.

Make 8

Step 3 With right sides together, position 1-1/2-inch **BEIGE** squares on the corners of a 1-1/2 x 5-1/2-inch **RUST** rectangle. Draw a diagonal line on the squares; stitch, trim, and press.

Make 8

Step 4 With right sides together, position a 1-1/2-inch **BEIGE** square on the corner of a 1-1/2 x 2-1/2-inch **BLACK** rectangle. Draw a diagonal line on the square; stitch, trim, and press. Repeat this process at the opposite corner of the rectangle. Make 4 units. Sew 1-1/2 x 2-1/2-inch **BEIGE** rectangles to both side edges of each unit; press. At this point each unit should measure 1-1/2 x 6-1/2-inches.

Make 4

Make 4

Step 5 Referring to the block diagram, sew together the Step 1, Step 2, and Step 3 units; press. Make 4 units. Sew the Step 4 units to the top edge of each unit; press. At this point each pumpkin block should measure 6-1/2-inches square.

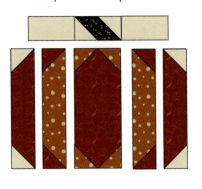 

Make 4

Step 6 Referring to the quilt diagram on page 89, sew together the leaf blocks and the pumpkin blocks in 3 rows. Press the seam allowances in alternating directions by rows so the seams will fit snugly together with less bulk. Sew the rows together; press. At this point the quilt center should measure 18-1/2-inches square.

borders

*Note: The yardage given allows for the border strips to be cut on the crosswise grain. Read through **Border** instructions on page 100 for general instructions on adding borders.*

Cutting

From **BLACK PRINT**:
- Cut 2, 1 x 42-inch inner border strips

From **BEIGE PRINT**:
- Cut 2, 1 x 42-inch middle border strips

From **GREEN PRINT**:
- Cut 3, 3-1/2 x 42-inch outer border strips

Attaching the Borders

Step 1 Attach the 1-inch wide **BLACK** inner border strips.

Step 2 Attach the 1-inch wide **BEIGE** middle border strips.

Step 3 Attach the 3-1/2-inch wide **GREEN** outer border strips.

putting it all together

Trim the backing and batting so they are 6-inches larger than the quilt top. Refer to **Finishing the Quilt** on page 100 for complete instructions. Our quilt was machine quilted with an allover quilt design.

binding

Cutting

From **BLACK PRINT**:
- Cut 3, 2-3/4 x 42-inch strips

Sew the binding to the quilt using a 3/8-inch seam allowance. This measurement will produce a 1/2-inch wide finished double binding. Refer to **Binding** and **Diagonal Piecing** on page 101 for complete instructions.

Place lots of pumpkins throughtout your home

for a harvest welcome.

This colorful fall arrangement will warm any room.

General Instructions

Getting Started

• Yardage is based on 42-inch wide fabric. If your fabric is wider or narrower it will affect the amount of necessary strips you need to cut in some patterns, and of course, it will affect the amount of fabric you have leftover. Generally, THIMBLEBERRIES patterns allow for a little extra fabric so you can confidently cut your pattern pieces with ease.

• A rotary cutter, mat, and wide clear plastic ruler with 1/8-inch markings are needed tools in attaining accuracy. A beginner needs good tools just as an experienced quiltmaker needs good equipment. A 24 x 36-inch mat board is a good size to own. It will easily accommodate the average quilt fabrics and will aid in accurate cutting. The plastic ruler you purchase should be at least 6 x 24-inches and easy to read. Do not purchase a smaller ruler to save money, the large size will be invaluable to your quiltmaking success.

• It is often recommended to prewash and press fabrics to test for colorfastness and possible shrinkage. If you choose to prewash, wash in cool water and dry in a cool to moderate dryer. Industry standards actually suggest that line drying is best. Shrinkage is generally very minimal and usually is not a concern. A good way to test your fabric for both shrinkage and colorfastness is to cut a 3-inch square of fabric. Soak the fabric in a white bowl filled with water. Squeeze the water out of the fabric and press it dry on a piece of muslin. If the fabric is going to release color it will do so either in the water or when it is pressed dry. Re-measure the 3-inch fabric square to see if it has changed size considerably (more than 1/4-inch). If it has, wash, dry, and press the entire yardage. This little test could save you hours in prewashing and pressing.

• Read instructions thoroughly before beginning a project. Each step will make more sense to you when you have a general overview of the whole process. Take one step at time and follow the illustrations. They will often make more sense to you than the words.

• For piecing, place right sides of the fabric pieces together and use 1/4-inch seam allowances throughout the entire quilt unless otherwise specifically stated in the directions. An accurate seam allowance is the most important part of the quiltmaking process after accurate cutting. All the directions are based on accurate 1/4-inch seam allowances. It is very important to check your sewing machine to see what position your fabric should be to get accurate seams. To test, use a piece of 1/4-inch graph paper, stitch along the quarter inch line as if the paper where fabric. Make note of where the edge of the paper lines up with your presser foot or where it lines up on the throat plate of your machine. Many quilters place a piece of masking tape on the throat plate to help guide the edge of the fabric. Now test your seam allowance on fabric. Cut 2, 2-1/2-inch squares, place right sides together and stitch along one edge. Press seam allowances in one direction and measure. At this point the unit should measure 2-1/2 x 4-1/2-inches. If it does not, adjust your stitching guidelines and test again. Seam allowances are included in the cutting sizes given in this book.

• Pressing is the third most important step in quiltmaking. As a general rule, you should never cross a stitched seam with another seam unless it has been pressed. Therefore, every time you stitch a seam it needs to be pressed before adding another piece. Often, it will feel like you press as much as you sew, and often that is true. It is very important that you press and not iron the seams. Pressing is a firm, up and down motion that will flatten the seams but not distort the piecing. Ironing is a back and forth motion and will stretch and distort the small pieces. Most quilters use steam to help the pressing process. The moisture does help and will not distort the shapes as long as the pressing motion is used.

• An old fashioned rule is to press seam allowances in one direction, toward the darker fabric. Often, background fabrics are light in color and pressing toward the darker fabric prevents the seam allowances from showing through to the right side. Pressing seam allowances in one direction is thought to create a stronger seam. Also, for ease in hand-quilting, the quilting lines should fall on the side of the seam which is opposite the seam allowance. As you piece quilts, you will find these "rules" to be helpful but not necessarily always appropriate. Sometimes seams need to be pressed in the opposite direction so the seams of different units will fit together more easily which quilters refer to as seams "nesting" together. When sewing together two units with opposing seam allowances, use the tip of your seam ripper to gently guide the units under your presser foot. Sometimes it is necessary to re-press the seams to make the units fit together nicely. Always try to achieve the least bulk in one spot and accept that no matter which way you press, it may be a little tricky and it could be a little bulky.

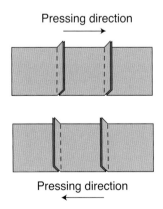

Pressing direction

Pressing direction

Squaring Up Blocks

To square up your blocks, first check the seam allowances. This is usually where the problem is, and it is always best to alter within the block rather than trim the outer edges. Next, make sure you have pressed accurately. Sometimes a block can become distorted by ironing instead of pressing.

• To trim up block edges, use one of many clear plastic squares available on the market. Determine the center of the block; mark with a pin. Lay the square over the block and align as many perpendicular and horizontal lines as you can to the seams in your block. This will indicate where the block is off. Do not trim all off on one side; this usually results in real distortion of the pieces in the block and the block design. Take a little off all sides until the block is square. When assembling many blocks, it it necessary to make sure *all* are the same size.

Tools and Equipment

Making beautiful quilts does not require a large number of specialized tools or expensive equipment. My list of favorites is short and sweet, and includes the things I use over and over again because they are always accurate and dependable.

• I find a long acrylic ruler indispensable for accurate rotary cutting. The ones I like most are an Omnigrid 6 x 24-inch grid acrylic ruler for cutting long strips and squaring up fabrics and quilt tops, and a Masterpiece 45, 8 x 24-inch ruler for cutting 6- to 8-inch wide borders. I sometimes tape together two 6 x 24-inch acrylic rulers for cutting borders up to 12-inches wide.

• A 15-inch Omnigrid square acrylic ruler is great for squaring up individual blocks and corners of a quilt top, for cutting strips up to 15-inches wide or long, and for trimming side and corner triangles.

• The markings on a 23 x 35-inch Olfa rotary cutting mat stay visible longer than on other mats, and the lines are fine and accurate.

• The largest size Olfa rotary cutter cuts through many layers of fabric easily, and it isn't cumbersome to use. The 2-1/2-inch blade slices through three layers of backing, batting, and a quilt top like butter.

• An 8-inch pair of Gingher shears is great for cutting out applique templates and cutting fabric from a bolt or fabric scraps.

• I keep a pair of 5-1/4-inch Gingher scissors by my sewing machine, so it is handy for both machine work and handwork. This size is versatile and sharp enough to make large and small cuts equally well.

• My Grabbit magnetic pin cushion has a surface that is large enough to hold lots of straight pins, and a strong magnet that keeps them securely in place.

• Silk pins are long and thin, which means they won't leave large holes in your fabric. I like them because they increase accuracy in pinning pieces or blocks together, and it is easy to press over silk pins, as well.

• For pressing individual pieces, blocks, and quilt tops, I use an 18 x 48-inch sheet of plywood covered with several layers of cotton fiberfill and topped with a layer of muslin stapled to the back. The 48-inch length allows me to press an entire width of fabric at one time without the need to reposition it, and the square ends are better than tapered ends on an ironing board for pressing finished quilt tops.

Rotary Cutting

• **Safety First!** The blades of a rotary cutter are very sharp and need to be for accurate cutting. Look at a variety of cutters to find one that feels good in your hand. All quality cutters have a safety mechanism to "close" the cutting blade when not in use. After each cut and before laying the rotary cutter down, close the blade. Soon this will become second nature to you and will prevent dangerous accidents. Always keep cutters out of the sight of children. Rotary cutters are very tempting to fiddle with when they are laying around. When your blade is dull or nicked, change it. Damaged blades do not cut accurately and require extra effort that can also result in slipping and injury. Also, always cut away from yourself for safety.

• Fold the fabric in half lengthwise matching the selvage edges.

• "Square off" the ends of your fabric before measuring and cutting pieces. This means that the cut edge of the fabric must be exactly perpendicular to the folded edge which creates a 90° angle. Align the folded and selvage edges of the fabric with the lines on the cutting board, and place a ruled square on the fold. Place a 6 x 24-inch ruler against the

side of the square to get a 90° angle. Hold the ruler in place, remove the square, and cut along the edge of the ruler. If you are left-handed, work from the other end of the fabric. Use the lines on your cutting board to help line up fabric, but not to measure and cut strips. Use a ruler for accurate cutting, always checking to make sure your fabric is lined up with horizontal and vertical lines on the ruler.

6" x 24" ruler

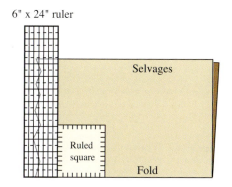

Selvages

Ruled square

Fold

Cutting Strips

• When cutting strips or rectangles, cut on the crosswise grain. Strips can then be cut into squares or smaller rectangles.

• If your strips are not straight after cutting a few of them, refold the fabric, align the folded and selvage edges with the lines on the cutting board, and "square off" the edge again by trimming to straighten, and begin cutting.

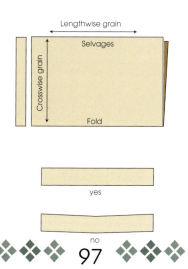

Lengthwise grain

Selvages

Crosswise grain

Fold

yes

no

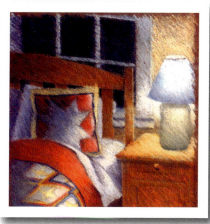

Cutting Side and Corner Triangles

In projects with side and corner triangles, the instructions have you cut side and corner triangles larger than needed. This will allow you to square up the quilt and eliminates the frustration of ending up with precut side and corner triangles that don't match the size of your pieced blocks.

• To cut triangles, first cut squares. The project directions will tell you what size to make the squares and whether to cut them in half to make two triangles or to cut them in quarters to make four triangles, as shown in the diagrams. This cutting method will give you side triangles that have the straight of grain on the outside edges of the quilt. This is a very important part of quilt making that will help stabilize your quilt center.

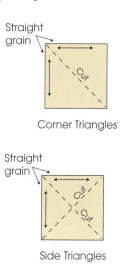

Straight grain

Cut

Corner Triangles

Straight grain

Cut

Cut

Side Triangles

Trimming Side and Corner Triangles

Begin at a corner by lining up your ruler 1/4-inch beyond the points of the corners of the blocks as shown. Cut along the edge of the ruler. Repeat this procedure on all four sides of the quilt top.

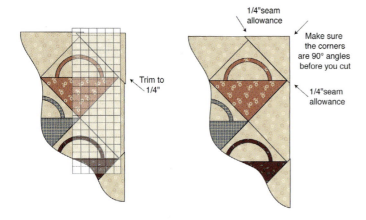

Accurate Triangles

Stitch on the outer edge just a "hair" or a thread width from the marked diagonal line.

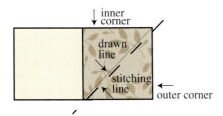

If you stitch on the inner corner side of the diagonal line you will actually make the triangle smaller.

"Square" Strip Sets

Make a habit of stopping often to check that your ruler is perpendicular to the strip set as you crosscut your segments. Lining up a horizontal marking on your ruler with a strip set seam will help keep your segments "square."

Pressing Strip Sets

When sewing strips of fabric together for strip sets, it is important to press the seam allowances nice and flat, usually to the dark fabric. Be careful not to stretch as you press, causing a "rainbow effect." This will affect the accuracy and shape of the pieces cut from the strip set. Press on the wrong side first with the strips perpendicular to the ironing board. Flip the piece over and press on the right side to prevent little pleats from forming at the seams. Laying the strip set lengthwise on the ironing board seems to encourage the rainbow effect, as shown in diagram.

Avoid this "rainbow effect"

Quilting Suggestions

• Repeat one of the design elements in the quilt as part of the quilting design.

• Two or three parallel rows of echo quilting outside an applique piece will highlight the shape.

• Stipple or meander quilting behind a feather or central motif will make the primary design more prominent.

• Look for quilting designs that will cover two or more borders, rather than choosing separate designs for each individual border.

• Quilting in-the-ditch of seams is an effective way to get a project quilted without a great deal of time marking the quilt.

Chain Piecing

To make the piecing process for "Radiant Star" more efficient, plan on chain piecing the "triangles" at one time. Clip, trim, and press; then repeat for the opposite corner of the rectangle.

Marking the Quilt Design

When marking the quilt top, use a marking tool that will be visible on the quilt fabric and yet will be easy enough to remove. Always test your marking tool on a scrap of fabric before marking the entire quilt.

Along with a multitude of commercial marking tools available, you may find that very thin slivers of hand soap (Dial, Ivory, etc.) work really well for marking medium to dark color fabrics. The thin lines of soap show up nicely and they are easily removed by simply rubbing gently with a piece of like-colored fabric.

To remove the blue lines of water erasable markers, refer to the manufacturer's directions before laundering or pressing your finished quilt. Do not iron over the marked lines before removing. Ironing markings on some materials will set the marks permanently.

Borders

Note . . .

The diagonal seams disguise the piecing better than straight seams. The exception is when a woven plaid is used for a border. It is then best to cut the border strips on the lengthwise grain (parallel to the selvages). When sewing on the bias, sew slowly and do not use too small of a stitch which could cause stretching of the fabric.

Diagonal Piecing

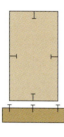

Stitch diagonally   Trim to 1/4" seam allowance   Press seam open

Step 1   With pins, mark the center points along all 4 sides of the quilt. For the top and bottom borders, measure the quilt from left to right through the middle. This measurement will give you the most accurate measurement that will result in a "square" quilt.

Step 2   Measure and mark the border lengths and center points on the strips cut for the borders before sewing them on.

Step 3   Pin the border strips to the quilt matching the pinned points on each of the borders and the quilt. Pin borders every 6 to 8-inches easing the fabric to fit as necessary. This will prevent the borders and quilt center from stretching while you are sewing them together. Stitch a 1/4-inch seam. Press the seam allowance toward the borders. Trim off excess border lengths.

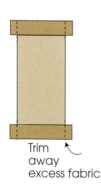

Trim away excess fabric

Step 4   For the side borders, measure your quilt from top to bottom, including the borders just added, to determine the length of the side borders.

Step 5   Measure and mark the side border lengths as you did for the top and bottom borders.

Step 6   Pin and stitch the side border strips in place. When attaching the last two side outer border strips, taking a few backstitches at the beginning and the end of the border will help keep the quilt borders intact during the quilting process.   Press and trim the border strips even with the borders just added.

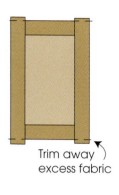

Trim away excess fabric

Step 7   If your quilt has multiple borders, measure, mark, and sew additional borders to the quilt in the same manner.

Finishing the Quilt

Now that your quilt top is finished it needs to be layered with batting and backing, and prepared for quilting. Whether it is machine-quilted or hand-quilted, it is best to baste all 3 layers together. You may hand-baste with large basting stitches or pin-baste with medium size brass safety pins. Many quilters are satisfied with spray adhesives which are available at local quilt shops.

Step 1 Press the completed quilt top on the backside first, carefully clipping and removing hanging threads. Then press the quilt front making sure all seams are flat and all loose threads are removed.

Step 2 Remove the selvages from the backing fabric. Sew the long edges together; press. Trim the backing and batting so they are 4-inches larger than the quilt top.

Step 3 Mark the quilt top for quilting. Layer the backing, batting, and quilt top. Baste the 3 layers together and quilt. Work from the center of the quilt out to the edges. This will help keep the quilt flat by working the excess of the 3 layers to the outside edges.

Step 4 When quilting is complete, remove basting. Hand-baste the 3 layers together a scant 1/4-inch from the edge. This basting keeps the layers from shifting and prevents puckers from forming when adding the binding. Trim excess batting and backing fabric even with the edge of the quilt top.

Cutting Bias Binding

To cut bias binding strips, fold the binding yardage on the diagonal, forming a triangle. Using a rotary cutter, mat, and wide acrylic ruler, measure 1/2-inch from the fold, and cut away the folded edge to get a cut straight edge. Move the ruler across the fabric, cutting parallel strips in the desired binding width.

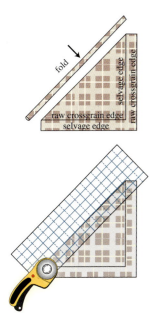

Diagonally piece the bias binding strips together, using as many long strips as possible, with shorter strips placed between the longer strips. Be careful not to stretch the seams as you stitch binding strips together.

Diagonal Piecing

in diagonally   Trim to 1/4" seam   Press seam open
                 allowance

The instructions for each quilt indicate the width to cut the binding used in that project. The measurements are sufficient for a quilt made of cotton fabrics and medium low loft quilt batting. If you use a high loft batt or combine a fluffy high loft batt with flannel fabrics, you may want to increase the width of the binding strips by adding 1/4 to 1/2-inch to the cut width of your binding. Always test a small segment of the binding before cutting all the strips needed.

Step 1 Diagonally piece the binding strips. Fold the strip in half lengthwise, wrong sides together; press.

Double-Layer Binding

Step 2 Unfold and trim one end at a 45° angle. Turn under the edge 1/4-inch; press. Refold the strip.

Fold Line

Step 3 With raw edges of the binding and quilt top even, stitch with a 3/8-inch seam allowance, unless otherwise specified, starting 2-inches from the angled end.

Step 4 Miter the binding at the corners. As you approach a corner of the quilt, stop sewing 3/8 to 1-inch from the corner of the quilt (use the same measurement as your seam allowance). Generally, a 3/8-inch seam allowance is used for regular cotton quilts and often a 1-inch seam allowance is used for flannel quilts. Each project in this book gives specific instructions for the binding width and seam allowance to be used.

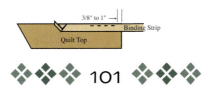

3/8" to 1"
Binding Strip
Quilt Top

Step 5 Clip the threads and remove the quilt from under the presser foot.

Step 6 Flip the binding strip up and away from the quilt, then fold the binding down even with the raw edge of the quilt. Begin sewing at the upper edge. Miter all 4 corners in this manner.

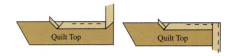

Quilt Top   Quilt Top

Step 7 Trim the end of the binding so it can be tucked inside of the beginning binding about 1/2-inch. Finish stitching the seam.

Quilt Top   Quilt Top

Step 8 Turn the folded edge of the binding over the raw edges and to the back of the quilt so that the stitching line does not show. The corners will naturally turn with very little effort. Pin as needed to create a nice mitered corner on the back as well as on the front. Slip stitch the binding to the backside of the quilt by hand. To do this, slip your needle into the quilt back, sliding the needle approximately 1/4-inch. Bring it out of the fabric again and catch a few threads in the fold of the binding. At exactly the same point from which the needle emerged, insert it into the quilt back again, and take the next stitch. It is a good idea to take a double stitch approximately every 6 to 8-inches to anchor the binding.

Quilt Back   Quilt Back   Quilt Back

Quilt Backing Basics

Yardage Requirements and Piecing Suggestions

Crib
45 x 60"

2-3/4 yards
Cut 2, 1-3/8 yard lengths

Twin
72 x 90"

5-1/3 yards
Cut 2, 2-2/3 yard lengths

Double/Full
81 x 96"

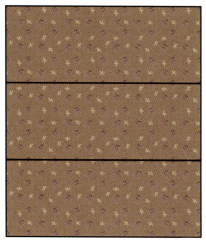

7-1/8 yards
Cut 3, 2-3/8 yard lengths

Queen
90 x 108"

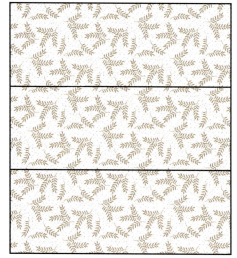

8 yards
Cut 3, 2-2/3 yard lengths

Rod Casing or Sleeve

To hang wall quilts, attach a casing that is made of the same fabric as the quilt back. Attach this casing at the top of the quilt, just below the binding. Often, it is helpful to attach a second casing at the bottom of the quilt so you can insert a dowel into it which will help weight the quilt and make it hang free of ripples.

To make a rod casing or "sleeve", cut enough strips of fabric equal to the width of the quilt plus 2-inches for side hems. Generally, 6-inch wide strips will accommodate most rods. If you are using a rod with a larger diameter, increase the width of the strips.

Seam the strips together to get the length needed; press. Fold the strip in half lengthwise, wrong sides together. Stitch the long raw edges together with a 1/4-inch seam allowance. Center the seam on the backside of the sleeve; press. The raw edges of the seam will be concealed when the sleeve is stitched to the back of the quilt. Turn under both of the short raw edges; press and stitch to hem the ends. The final measurement should be about 1/2-inch from the quilt edges.

Pin the sleeve to the back of the quilt so the top edge of the sleeve is just below the binding. Hand-stitch the top edge of the sleeve in place, then the bottom edge. Make sure to knot and secure your stitches at each end of the sleeve to make sure it will not pull away from the quilt with use. Slip the rod into the casing. If your wall quilt is not directional, making a sleeve for the bottom edge will allow you to turn your quilt end to end to relieve the stress at the top edge. You could also slip a dowel into the bottom sleeve to help anchor the lower edge of the wall quilt.

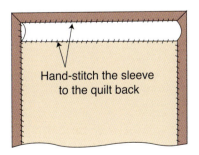

Hand-stitch the sleeve
to the quilt back

Pouncing the Quilting Design

After you've selected a quilting design, the Quilt Pounce™ makes it easy to transfer any size or variety of stencil to your quilt top. Simply fill the Quilt Pounce™ pad's large inner reservoir with the chalk powder (included) and gently wipe it across the surface of the stencil that has been positioned on the quilt top. Continue moving the stencil and "pouncing" the quilting design. Some white and blue chalks do not iron off - they brush/wash off. If you don't plan to wash your quilt, be sure to use the iron-off Ultimate Quilt Pounce™.

Tip: Keep your pressed and marked quilt top wrinkle-free by folding it wrong side out and hanging it from a skirt hanger.

Thimbleberries Quilting Stencils

Ask at your local quilt shop for Thimbleberries quilt stencils by Quilting Creations International or visit www.quiltingcreations.com

Thimbleberries offers a complete line of patterns, books and fabric for quilts and creative home accessories.
For more information, visit our website at www.thimbleberries.com.

Thimbleberries, Inc.
7 North Main Street
Hutchinson, MN 55350

Thank you to the
Staff of Thimbleberries® Design Studio

Sue Bahr • Lisa Kirchoff • Ardelle Paulson
Sherry Husske • Virginia Brodd
Julie Jergens • Renae Ashwill

Contributing Stitchers
Clarine Howe • Amy Albrecht
Leone Rusch • Connie Albin
Beth Rakow